LAST OF THE
SMALL
TOWNS

LAST OF THE
SMALL
TOWNS

——————— Short Stories ———————

STEWART HYSON

ARPress
45 Dan Road Suite 5
Canton MA 02021

Hotline: 1(800) 220-7660
Fax: 1(855) 752-6001

Ordering Information:
Quantity sales. Special discounts are available on quantity purchases by corporations, associations, and others. For details, contact the publisher at the address above.

Printed in the United States of America.

ISBN-13:   Paperback   979-8-89389-890-3
                 eBook   979-8-89389-891-0

Library of Congress Control Number: 2024923849

CONTENTS

PREFACE

y hometown – Hantsport, Nova Scotia – where I grew-up during the 1950s and early '60s no longer exists. Now be careful with how you read the preceding sentence – do not read it literally, word for word. After all, there is still physically a place called Hantsport; just take a quick break to "Google" the name on the Internet. Second, I am not simply referring to the fact that Hantsport's legal status, at the time of writing, had been recently changed from that of a fully incorporated town to that of only being a speck of dust in the spacious and amorphous district of West Hants.

So I am not quibbling about Hantsport's physical presence or its legal status by stating that the town no longer exists. I am instead taking a much broader, figurative perspective by saying that there was a different Hantsport during the 1950s and early '60s. Hantsport's residents at that time had a distinctive swagger not found before or since. The pattern of life was that of a bustling, hard-working and successful people. We were proud and comfortable with ourselves, satisfied with what the community had accomplished, and optimistic about the future. Looking back through the fog of time, we see a community that had originally been founded upon the building of wooden ships during the 1800s and then had morphed by mid-20th century into a tightly knit town based economically on several small-scaled industries. By the post-World War II years, Hantsport was at its zenith of activity and prosperity – a distinctive hometown that is still fondly remembered and cherished.

The community has since declined, not unlike so many other communities, and has even lost its legal distinction of being a town. By the way, in order to fill the knowledge gap for the average reader, Hantsport had been incorporated as a town in 1895 but then lost this status on July 1, 2015. My prime intent is not to comment on this demise. Nor do I intend to speculate on whether Hantsport can or will re-invent itself in the near future. Rather, the goal is instead to portray the town as it used to be. This book is an account of childhood memories of growing up in Hantsport during the '50s and early '60s that are presented in the format of short stories.

In a way, these stories are like an archaeological dig probing the way of life of an earlier time. Like unpeeling one at a time the layers of an onion, each short story portrays via boyhood adventures how kids developed to identify with their community. This begs the question: what was Hantsport like during the '50s and early '60s? Accordingly, the short stories are preceded by a "Background Information" section that sets the scene by physically describing the town and its people as they used to be. Then the short stories focus on childhood activities to describe the pattern of life in the last of the small towns.

Rather than present a chronological account, the short story format was chosen because it allows for greater creative interpretation and presentation, and provides a more entertaining read. .Humour is incorporated as much as possible in these short stories, with occasional references to popular songs and cartoons of the era as well as to games and goofing around. On occasion, readers are encouraged to Google items on the Internet or listen to the music of the era. Some common informal – but not vulgar or obscene – wording and phrasing are occasionally used in order to be more realistic if not to add spice to the story. Life was fun in the '50s and early '60s, and should be depicted that way. We were kids after all – not angels and not necessarily hellions, but rather good-natured rascals!

It would be unforgivable of me not to mention several friends who proof-read earlier versions of this manuscript to improve its readability, or who provided other stylistic advice: Jim Hooper, Duncan Gray, David Creelman, Jim McAllister, Greg Cook, and Don Desserud. In addition, factual gaps in my memory were filled by my good friend, Brian Bishop, as well as by my late mother (Kathleen), my brothers (Graham and Kempton), and my sister (Pamela). Finally, I read several books – as listed in the annotated bibliography – in order to refresh my factual memory of Hantsport, Annapolis Valley, Nova Scotia and its people. Any remaining errors, however, remain my fault and reflect my imperfect memory – hey, I am only human after all.

BACKGROUND INFORMATION

These background remarks are intended to set the scene for the short stories that follow by describing the physical features of Hantsport and its residents during the 1950s and early '60s.

Hantsport during the 1950s and early '60s: Physical Description

Hantsport was a town whose main street was a true Main Street which was the hub of activity, especially on Saturday nights. People would come from near and far to do their weekly shopping, take in a movie or ball-game, attend a dance, or simply to drive by – either to see the sights or to be seen driving by. Although I do not remember any neon lights and we were a long way from being a city, Petula Clark's 1965 hit song, *Downtown*, still accurately captured the flavour of Hantsport's reality at that time. To paraphrase Clark's lyrics, no matter how lonely we were, nor the troubles that haunted us, kids were attracted to the lights, noise and hurry of Hantsport's Saturday night on Main Street where we could feel happy (even if we only had our 25 cent weekly allowance in the pocket).

There were numerous businesses found on that front of Main Street stretching from the corner of Main and William Streets to the intersection of Main, Prince and School Streets. With little effort, I can easily recall two grocery stores, a pharmacy, a department store, two gas and garage service stations, and an electrical goods store with a professional electrician on call, two hardware stores, one of the town's two banks, a jeweler, two or three clothing stores, a taxi operator, a restaurant and motel, and at least one hairdresser and one barber.

Elsewhere scattered throughout the town were a movie theatre, a Sears catalogue order and pick-up store, a pool hall, a reading room and book store, four churches each with an active congregation, two or three family-owned pop, candy and magazine convenience stores, Post Office, town hall with attached police office and fire hall, a third grocery store, a second bank, a train station and a telegraph operator, two doctor offices, at least two other small restaurants, and additional barbers and hairdressers. It was a time when buses went through town several times a day, as did passenger, ore, and freight trains. A new school with its own attached gym was opened in 1961 in response to anticipated educational needs; it was also a time when an outdoor swimming pool, tennis court, and playground facilities were built on the Community Centre grounds.

The town was truly a "town of industries" which was the message on the highway sign that welcomed residents, visitors and passersby. The industries included a lumber and fruit basket making factory, gypsum ore loading port facility, apple juice cannery, pulp-making plant with its own port facility, molded pulp plate and egg carton making factory, and a candy factory. Numerous other industries had existed in previous times going back to the ship-building days of the 1800s, but they had fallen by the wayside by the post-World War II years. As only kids can do, we turned many of these industrial sites into theme parks for play, as in the case of the "Funny-Book Shed" or simply walking along the railroad tracks towards "Indian Graveyard" (as depicted in the short stories). I suppose that it was a bit risky playing so close to industrial machines but we were never worried, and were seldom injured.

Besides these built-up areas, there were wooded green areas and open fields for fun and games, not to mention the Avon River beach and fishing locations plus other ponds and water areas. Throughout the town were also cherry, apple, and pear trees as well as small fruit bushes that we regularly raided. Hantsport's senior-level baseball team (the *Shamrocks*) was so popular and successful that players came from across the province to play for it (see Brian Bishop's 2015 book listed in the bibliography that details the history of baseball in Hantsport). Meanwhile, quiet side streets existed in such numbers to allow street-hockey games at anytime of day. While recognizing these features of the town and all of the town's accomplishments by the middle of the 20th century, we must keep in mind that Hantsport had a remarkably small population, usually in the 1200 – 1400 range at most. The small size allowed everybody to know each other and to forge a common identity.

Perhaps of equal if not greater interest was the fact that Hantsport was also on the cusp of change like so many other communities at the time. The town was not stuck in the mud, reliant upon its past laurels, but we embraced change. Oh, certainly, it was not uncommon to see horse-drawn wagons delivering groceries, or to observe adult men doff their hats or touch the hat brim as they passed a woman on a sidewalk. But even these old-fashioned practices were quickly disappearing as the fifties rolled along. The natural urge, however, was to recognize and warmly welcome change – this was, after all, the Sputnik Era (the "space race" was ushered in with the launch of the Russian *Sputnik* satellite in 1957), and technological change was the name of the game! We were excited and loved these changes..

Ships from distant locations came for loads of either gypsum ore or bales of pulp. A side consequence was that the ship crews introduced the town's people to both different commercial products (*Tootsie* roll candies and *Camel* cigarettes, for example) and different cultural artifacts, such as chopsticks and a strange yet simple game called soccer. Television may have contributed to the closure of the local movie theatre, but it also opened our eyes to the world beyond our town's borders. Refrigerators replaced iceboxes and the ice delivery business. Not only did refrigerators put an end to the weekly chore of carrying (and spilling) the melted ice water to the kitchen sink, they also allowed ice cream to stay properly frozen until eaten. Trucks and cars along with an improved highway system spelled the eventual downfall of the passenger train service and train mail delivery, yet they made getting around so much easier. Instead of the old two-hour trip to the major city of Halifax, it now takes about 45 minutes. The opening of large super-markets and shopping-malls in larger, neighbouring communities sucked away the life support of the town's small businesses, but made a greater variety of goods available that were less expensive. Change was thus a welcomed phenomenon.

It is one thing to describe the physical features of Hantsport during the '50s and early '60s to get a handle for what constituted a real small town of yesterday. But what can we say about its people who were the town's life and blood? Who were the children growing up in the town at that time?

Identification: Who We Were

This collection of short stories is primarily about how kids grew up in Hantsport during the 1950s and early 1960s. We were of the baby-boom generation, although that term was never part of our vocabulary. On the one hand, we enjoyed the comfortable sense of community, long-standing traditions, and personal connections with older generations. Content with the constants of life – fishing on the river, trekking to Indian Graveyard, going to school, raiding apple and cherry trees whenever we had a taste, and playing every and all sporting games whenever we liked or building forts to have friendly snowball fights. Even the deaths of those close to us, allowed us to grieve together and thereby re-enforce that precious feeling of familiarity that nurtures a small town's identity. Yet, as suggested above, we also embraced change; for us, the future was without limits. From sailing off to Tahiti to make movies to travelling the world if not to outer space, dreams became expectations and then real possibilities. .

Most of the town's residents were Caucasian although there were a few black or African-Canadian families. Interestingly, every kid knew that the town's war cenotaph was dedicated to a former resident, William Hall, who was the first black to ever win the highest award for bravery in the British Empire (the *Victoria Cross*) at the Siege of Lucknow in 1857 during the Indian Rebellion (or Mutiny). (Here's another opportunity to Google the Internet for Hall's life story.) Meanwhile, I do not recall any families of Asian descent while growing up, and only a few First Nation children from a small reserve on the edge of the town. Thus, although racial differences were apparent, I was never aware of racist attitudes voiced by my crowd of friends.

Most family structures were typical for the time, headed by two parents: the male or husband/father who usually went out to work at a paying job each day and the woman or wife/mother who usually stayed home to manage the house and children. By the late 1960s, this pattern began to change as more married women were pursuing jobs outside of the home. My mother, for example, first established her own hairdressing business, and then she later started to work at the Sears catalogue order and pick-up store. Besides the typical family structure, however, there were a few single-parent families; headed by a working mother but we never gave these alternative family arrangements a second thought.

Families were mostly working-class families, although there were a few that were lower or upper middle class. Still, it bears stressing that R. A. Jodrey was the town's leading entrepreneur and was reputedly one of the wealthiest individuals in Nova Scotia if not all of Canada (Bruce 1981). I never knew him personally but often saw him walking by my home as he lived only a short distance away or he was going to one of his businesses. However, I did go to school with some of his grandchildren who never allowed their family's wealth interfere with how they fitted in with their playmates.

Personally, I was born on August 13, 1945 in an English castle named Hazlewood Castle that was being used as a maternity hospital in Tadcaster, Yorkshire, England. Well, go ahead and settle your curiosity by searching the Internet again – this castle has had diverse usages over the centuries since it was first recorded in the Domesday census of 1086. My birth father (Ronald) was a Canadian soldier and my mother (Kathleen) was a Tadcaster woman who had married in November 1944; then after returning to the battlefield, he was killed in Wilp, Holland, on April 16, 1945, to be reburied later at the Canadian War Cemetery in the Dutch community of Holten.

Eventually, when I was old enough to sail the "ocean blue" in 1946, my mother – as both a war bride and widow – took me to meet my deceased father's family in Bridgetown, Nova Scotia. We later sailed back to England in 1947 when I was two; and finally we returned to Nova Scotia again by ship when I was three in 1948. Yes, three crossings of the Atlantic Ocean but no "water miles" to show for it – just bouts of sea-sickness and one bout of measles or was it chicken pox? My mother then re-married in 1949 to my second father (Merrill), and the new family settled in Hantsport where I was raised with my to-be two younger brothers and sister. As I told my playmates at that time, I had two fathers, one in heaven and one here in Hantsport.

ON THE ART OF APPLE RAIDING

Hurtling along, bursting out of the apple orchard on each side of the highway. Coming from the east, there was probably no better location from which to view the charming uniqueness of Hantsport during the 1950s and early 1960s than from Highway #1 atop Mt. Denson. From the highway clearing amidst the apple orchard, a panorama of Hantsport stretched out before the eye to be appreciated. You could easily frame in your mind the scope of the whole town, from the mainly residential areas on the left and centre of your view, to the port on the Avon River and the more industrial areas on your right.

From the Mt. Denson orchard gateway, the highway continued gradually dipping down the mount to a small bridge across the Halfway River and then into the town of Hantsport. Within a few seconds, the Baptist Church fronted by a memorial cairn or cenotaph to William Hall, V. C. stood on guard at a road intersection, greeting all arrivals.

Highway #1 continued past the church but was re-named locally as Willow Street, a residential part of town. Or if you wished at the crossroads, you could turn left onto Holmes Hill, another largely residential area that also included the town's cemetery; this had been previously the original road into Hantsport for many decades. Of course, after coming all this way from wherever you came, it made little sense to continue straight ahead on Willow Street or to turn onto

Holmes Hill because both options would quickly take you out of the town. Thus, most people, being of an inquisitive or social nature, not to mention sound mind, would instead choose the third alternative at the crossroads by turning right onto the town's Main Street. This option took you to the retail outlets, services like the Post Office and train station, two banks, three other churches, and the industrial enterprises located mainly on or near the riverfront and railroad.

Actually, from the viewpoint of the Mt. Denson apple orchard, a person would not see all of Hantsport's specific attractions. In the summertime months especially, the town's details were often shrouded by Oak and Elm tree foliage but roof tops of more prominent buildings were evident as well as the town's general dimensions. Still, even strangers could sense from afar that the town possessed a storehouse of hidden treasures, while residents had actually tasted the town's delights. The apple juice plant was just one of Hantsport's jewels, where kids learned the art of apple raiding! Oops, let's use political correctness and call it "apple picking, Hantsport style."

The Mt. Denson apple orchard was not simply a wonderful spot from which to view Hantsport, but it was also an indicator that you were now in the Annapolis Valley, one of Canada's major apple producing regions. In terms of bragging rights, the neighbouring town of Windsor is often considered to be the eastern beginning of the Valley. As well, cartographers, geologists, and other earth scientists have their own respective technical definitions of the Valley's physical dimensions. But for most lay persons in the '50s and early '60s, the Valley started at this spot in Mt. Denson. This was where you began to see the Valley's apple orchards and, during the fall harvest season, smelled the fragrance of freshly picked apples. The apples produced at this and other near-by orchards were transported to be processed at Hantsport's Avon brand apple juice cannery that was located next to the train station just down the street from my home in Hantsport. Besides processing apple juice, the plant also provided the opportunity for us to learn the art of "apple raiding."

In early September of each year, our attention would turn by instinct to the apple juice plant. Apples would be brought from the Mt. Denson apple orchard and countless other orchards within driving distance. Tons of apples were dumped into large outdoor holding bins. I suppose that it was the crisp, cool air of autumn that alerted us to the fact that it was time to raid the apple bins. Thus, following school in the late afternoon, we would head for the Avon apple juice plant, and sometimes we took friends with us.

"Come this way," I said, "it is just down William Street around the corner of the Sears store, down Station Street."

"But are you sure," replied Peter, "I have never been here before."

"Sure," added Johnnie. "You guys from the other side of Main Street have a lot to learn. But this is the best way to approach the apple juice plant without being seen. We can't enter through the main entrance, but must be sneaky."

To which Laurie added, "We only have to walk first around the candy factory on Station Street and then down through the alley to get to the juice plant."

"Candy factory? What candy factory? I never knew there was a candy factory in Hantsport," responded Jan.

"Yeah, it is called *Yeaton's* although I think it is owned by the Johnson family on Avon Street," clarified Wray. "It is odd because the factory always seems to be closed and I have never seen anybody enter or leave the place. I believe that they used to be a lot busier many years ago."

"I think they now operate only on special occasions," observed Laurie, "to make those toffee and molasses candy kisses in individual waxy paper wrappers that are tossed to the crowd during the July 1st Dominion Day parade, and are also sold at Halloween time. Also, they make Christmas and Easter candy."

At the end of the short alley alongside the candy factory, there was a small broken wooden fence gate not much wider than a house door and not above shoulder height. Its presence posed no real barrier that couldn't be easily climbed over. In fact, its small size and broken structure invited trespassers. Once passed the fence, we were immediately faced by the apple bins that towered above us. Just as quickly, the worry warts from above Main Street were at it again.

"But isn't the taking of apples 'stealing'?" wondered Peter.

"No," Wray replied. "Taking apples from these apple bins is like raiding an apple orchard or a cherry tree. Apple raiding is just natural, and not evil like stealing. It's all free for the taking, well sort of."

In response to this exchange, I clarified the divine order of the matter. "God provided us with apple trees. Around here, apple trees are so plentiful that we all know that they serve one purpose. The trees grow apples, and apples have to be eaten. Since the apple juice plant has gone to the bother of bringing tons of apples to these outdoor holding bins, don't we have a solemn duty to contribute to the processing of the apples? It is all part of the grand scheme of life."

It may not have been a perfect argument, but, in the minds of pre-teen boys, it was a convincing argument. A most convincing argument that had no other option than to be accepted without question! Once assured of the situation with no lingering doubts, we all proceeded without hesitation.

The holding bins must have been at least eight to ten feet high and built upon a concrete floor. Each side of a bin was about ten to fifteen feet wide, with steel pipes to brace the bins at their corners and in the middle. The sides of these bins between the pipes consisted of vertically placed wooden boards that were slightly spaced apart, close enough to hold the apples but large enough for kids to wrap their fingers and toes around. This construction design was obviously intended to attract kids to the annual rite of apple raiding. One more piece of evidence that we were doing the right thing. So we were just reciprocating by fulfilling our part of the grand design.

Up and over the top we went and, once inside a bin, the enjoyment began. We started picking apples, Hantsport style. Each of us would pick up the first "best" apple that he saw. After the first bite, the apple would soon be discarded because Johnnie had noticed a bunch of McIntosh apples in another corner of the bin, and we would all crawl over in that new direction. After the next bite of the "best" McIntosh, Wray would notice a bunch of Red Delicious apples or Laurie would see Russets or Bishop Pippins in a neighbouring bin. Red, yellow, brown apples, the choices were endless. Even our uptown friends, Peter and Jan, were well into the game searching for their preferred choices.

We usually ignored the small apples and only went for the large and extra-large ones, even if we took just one bite of each apple. The large sizes were understandable because the apples came from mature, well established orchards that hadn't produced small apples in a decade or more. Small apples were a rarity except for crab apples, which were not anybody's favourite. As well, the large apples had benefited from the balanced mix of rain drops and sun rays that had fallen all summer long, and now the apple flesh was being kissed 24-hours a day by the crisp and cool autumn air. All are ideal growing conditions for apples.

The bins were built side-by-side, so there was no difficulty to scramble from one bin to the next. Some bins, however, were about a foot or so apart due to a canal in the concrete floor. Apples were released from the bottom of each bin into the canal. Forced water in this canal would then float the apples from the bins into the plant across the yard to be processed. In any case, it was easy to hop across this canal from one bin to a bin that had better looking choices.

Besides munching on apples, we spent time talking mostly about the apple juice plant. We knew that the plant produced apple juice as part of the Avon line of canned fruits and vegetables. But we did not know much else about the company, although we probably developed a life-long brand loyalty to Avon.

Peter nevertheless expressed a health concern, "Should we be climbing about the apples and taking bites if the apples are then going to be used for apple juice to be drunk by people?"

Wray clarified matters once again, "There is nothing to be worried about. The apples are first washed. Then the apples are squeezed for the juice which is pasteurized for human use."

I added, "A lot of these apples are windfall apples and some have bugs. They are not top quality eating apples, but are only squeezed for the juice. And then the pasteurization makes everything safe. It is just like the pasteurization of milk."

Our talk consisted mainly of speculative discussion dressed up as sure-fired knowledge – the usual kind of kid talk. Although we were not experts, we seemed to have enough information to get through discussions. And so the autumn afternoon passed leisurely as we sampled apples trying to find the one best apple of them all. That is not quite true because our apple picking and conversation would always come to an abrupt sudden end with the arrival of the plant manager!

The manager's arrival was accompanied with his familiar shout, "hey, you kids, get the heck out of there" (or words to that same effect). Still, although expected, the shout would always come as a jolt as it awoke us from the delight of our lazy afternoon past-time. The manager's shout was a signal for us to climb promptly down the board sides of the apple bins, in reverse to how we had arrived, and to run for it. High tail it, in other words. Of course, this was part and parcel of the challenge and fun of the apple raid, to be chased away.

On this particular day, however, the manager was not content to chase us off the cannery's property but he also continued pursuing us down William Street. It was a bit different, but not a great worry. As kids, we knew the secrets of running.

First there is normal, fast running. But when you are scared-to-death, and have to run faster, every kid knew what to do. Shift into a higher gear! Bear down, make your strides shorter, and pump your legs up-and-down, faster and harder than ever before. Pumping, pumping, faster, faster, harder, harder! It is only for a short time, to be faster than a speeding bullet and, once in that gear, nobody can catch you. It was one of the secrets of being a kid; it might be called "The Secrets of Scared-to-Death Running, 101." It was something that you were never taught; it was natural knowledge that you acquired when you moved along in life from age nine to age ten. The fact that the manager did not catch us or even came close was testimony to the soundness of this hidden wisdom.

"Wow, that was scary," uttered Peter as he tried to catch his breath.

"Yeah," said Jan, "I thought you said that it was okay to pick a few apples."

I replied, "It is okay most of the time except when the manager sees you. Then he has to chase you away. It's part of his job. But we can easily out-run him with little difficulty."

Admittedly, I wasn't being fully truthful but my words did serve the purpose of soothing Peter and Jan. There had been a few thorny problems in the past. That is to say, while our apple-picking raids had always been successful, this is not to say that everything had gone smoothly.

There was the occasion when our attention was directed away from the apples to a piece of machinery next to the bins. It was a mobile conveyor belt on a pair of wheels that could be taken to different spots and used as needed. In our eyes, however, it looked like a teeter-totter since the two ends of the conveyor belt could be tipped up and down over the wheels. So we went over to amuse ourselves by teeter-tottering. The manager, however, did not share our newly discovered source of amusement.

Once we had been chased away, Johnnie realized that he had lost his hat near the conveyor belt. This was a difficult situation. Johnnie could not go home and tell his mother how he had lost his hat; yet, we had never before returned to the plant on the same day after being chased away. It was only after we had summoned our collective nerve that we were able to sneak back as a group to the conveyor belt to retrieve Johnnie's hat. It was a dicey situation, we were most frightened, but it was something that had to be done. Loyalty to a friend in need trumped all else. Fortunately, we were not seen on this return trip and our hat retrieval mission was a success. The build-up for the return had been nerve-wrecking, but the end result had been anti-climactic.

Without question, however, the most serious incident was when Laurie slipped while scrambling down the side of an apple bin. Everything had gone smoothly up to this point, from climbing into the bins, sampling the apples, and then departing when the manager shouted at us. But then Laurie had slipped, and his wrist caught onto a metal hook on top of one of the steel pipes. He was hollering in pain, flapping around like an eel on the end of a fishing line.

As Laurie had been directly following me when he slipped, his feet began banging me on the head and shoulders. He was trying to gain foot support in order to push himself up and unhook his wrist from the hook. Eventually, after gaining some traction, Laurie managed to pull his wrist off the hook. Then with blood gushing, spraying and splashing all over the place, and in considerable shock and pain, he ran home for help. His mother attended to Laurie's immediate needs before he was stitched up at the doctor's office. The seriousness of this particular incident sort of took the "fun" element out of raiding the apple juice plant, but for only for a short time, as kids' memories are brief.

There was no need to burden our uptown friends about the hat and bloody wrist stories or other past incidents when things had gone slightly wrong. It would be far better, instead, to allow Peter and Jan to relish their thrill of the moment of having been scared to death and chased off the apple juice plant property. After all, the experience would now be part of their memory of apple picking Hantsport style.

HOME IN THE 'HOOD

boy's life at the time was very much centtred on exploring and discovering: whether it was venturing each day a bit further from home; learning how to climb cherry trees to pick cherries; finding the best wood to make bows and arrows; locating pop and beer bottles; digging tunnels; finding the ideal spots for fishing; or whatever. .With active minds, we were actively on the go all the time, constantly exploring at home and in the woodlands searching for new discoveries.

There were always things to do; "boredom" was not part of our vocabulary. Even on rainy days, we would chant the children's refrain, "rain, rain, go away, and come back another day." Then we would take up our crayons to colour pictures in a colouring book or play board games. At other times, we would tip over kitchen chairs in order to sit on the chair backs, pretending the chairs to be cars in a car race. There were no limits to the imagination; everything and anything could be a source of amusement.

On more pleasant days in the neighbourhood, we were always out and about. My 'hood, as I will call it, was the older part of town bounded roughly by the riverfront, William Street, Prince Street, and Main Street. It included industrial locations that became our playgrounds as well as three small patches of woodland. The 'hood also contained the train station and railroad tracks, the movie theatre, the Post Office,

Sears catalogue order and pick-up store, two banks, a small book store and reading room, Harvie's grocery store, Dowe's convenience store, Cozy Corner restaurant, a snow-coasting hill, and much more. In short, even if I write with a bit of bias, this was the most stimulating (and interesting) part of the town.

As a young family getting its feet on the ground, we initially lived in a couple of different up-stair apartment flats. Some of the earliest memories that I have of living in Hantsport were when my family lived in an apartment unit of a two-storied house at 31 Prince Street between 1949 and 1953. Later as the family expanded, my parents acquired the house at 43 William Street, about mid-way between the railroad tracks and Davison Street near the riverfront. This was my prime homestead in the 'hood during the time that I experienced most of my memories of growing up in Hantsport.

a. Woodlands

It is interesting to observe human behaviour. First, as babies, we crawl adventurously from room to room to better know our home. Later, as we leave home, we travel a bit further away from home with each passing day. This allows us to better identify the signposts of our neighbourhood. We develop first a connection with the local people, buildings, streets, attractions, fields of play, and activities before venturing too far further away.

As we soon discovered, our 'hood contained three patches of woodland. The closest was where the town's fire station is now (in 2017) located. This woodland contained a couple of shortcut pathways. One went from our Prince Street apartment towards Harvie's grocery and Dowe's convenience stores on William Street as well as to the movie theatre, Post Office, Sears, train station, and two banks. So this woodland shortcut became a well-travelled pathway.

Besides its pathways, this woodland proved to be a favourite spot to play "Cowboys and Indians" or to simply run around or to hide out. We also learned to climb a couple of wild cherry trees for a feast when cherries were in season. At other times, we would cut thin, young trees to make fishing poles or bows and arrows.

Right next to this patch of woods was a hill. Apparently, this hill had once been a dirt road but I never saw it used by vehicles. This hill extended from my Prince Street apartment building down to the town hall which was then on William Street. The hill had a gentle slope that was ideal for coasting in winter time. Small individual sleds, three-to-five seat toboggans, and a larger, heavy duty bob-sleigh for six to eight passengers were all used. We coasted every winter evening with tremendous glee. Sometimes, it was possible in the right conditions to slide all the way to the town hall on William Street!

A second patch of woods was further away and was less frequented. It was on the edge of town at the end of Porter's Avenue and beside the Community Centre. It was just off the bank of the Halfway River with Mt. Denson on the other side of the river. Other than being a spacious spot in which to run around and hide, this woodland had little attraction or use for children.

By far, the most attractive patch of woods, however, was between the Avon apple juice plant and Tannery Road, and alongside the railroad tracks. This was a truly fascinating place not only to play in, but to explore. All of the trees were clumps of alder or willow trees – but I am no expert on tree identification – on land that was often wet and swampy. The tree growth was so thick that you could easily lose your sense of direction, at least for a brief moment. Actually, being momentarily lost, added to the suspenseful appeal of this thicket of woodland.

In spring time, this wooded area was usually flooded. So we learned to build rafts and then attempted to pole ourselves through the swampy tree clumps. Our efforts were similar to what we had seen in some jungle-located movies. Also, one of the *Davey Crockett* television episodes produced for television by Walt Disney in the mid-1950s had been about poling rafts on rivers, so we had added incentive to do likewise. However, our efforts to emulate what we had seen were usually less successful. I doubt if anybody survived a spring without getting their feet soaked at least once in the icy cold water – I still shiver from thinking about slipping a foot into that icy coldness!

We also went to this particular wooded area to cut thin, young trees and branches in order to make bows and arrows. These trees were better quality for this purpose with just the right thickness and flexibility for bows and arrows. On yet other occasions, we would cut a tree with two opposite branches and whittle it into a "Y" shape. Then by attaching rubber strips from an inner tire tube and a leather tongue from an old shoe, we made a sling shot.

At other times, we attempted to make whistles. But I am afraid that we lacked the know-how to succeed at this ancient practice of tree branch whistle-making.

Once when we were cutting branches for one purpose or another, Laurie was practicing his knife-throwing technique. He tossed his jack knife through the air, to stick the pointed end into the target – on this occasion, an old, abandoned wooden barrel.

Laurie: "Darn, I missed again. The knife did not stick; it just bounced off. Is it better to hold and throw the knife by the handle or by the blade end?"

Stewart: "No, I prefer to use the blade end. But, you must be careful not to cut yourself."

Johnnie: "I don't know. I usually fail no matter how I throw the knife."

In any case, when he went to retrieve his knife, Laurie found an unopened cardboard carton that contained bags of potato chips inside the barrel. We took the carton to Chief Allard at the police office. Apparently, the chips had been stolen from the train station located next to the woods, and then hidden by the thief or thieves in the barrel. Unfortunately, there was no reward of free chips for doing our good deed.

These woodlands were immediately accessible, and provided endless hours of play opportunity. Not just to play, but to grow and develop, to explore and to discover, to satisfy our natural inquisitiveness, and to become independent and self-reliant.

b. The Homestead

Our pursuit of exploration and discovery was never solely confined to wooded areas or elsewhere out-and-about. Much of our time was also focused on our house, barn and property grounds on William Street. The house and barn were older structures apparently built by a sea captain at the turn of the 20th century, so the rumour went. Meanwhile, the grounds were bordered by grape vines, a few cherry trees, rose bushes, popular and elm trees plus an oak tree.

Every fall, the giant oak tree at the corner of our homestead would shower the front lawn with acorns. This would spark our imaginations to create pretend "smoking pipes." Even though we never smoked, we would punch a hole in the side of an acorn by using a hammer and nail or the pointed end of a jack knife. Then we would stick a wooden match stick (or a tooth pick) into the hole. Presto, we had a pretend pipe just like those used by some of our fathers – once again, there were no limits to our imagination.

Speaking of nuts, we would also get chestnuts in the fall from somewhere else because there was no chestnut tree on the homestead. We used to play the ancient – mainly British, I believe – game of "conkers." (The term may be searched online for additional information.) We would punch a hole through each chestnut by again using a hammer and nail in order to draw through and attach a piece of thick string. Then each player in turn would swing his chestnut against an opponent's chestnut. The first player to smash to smithereens a targeted nut won.

Meanwhile, during the spring and early summer, we were attracted to the cherry trees that we would climb to pick cherries. I don't know the name of the variety of cherries that grew on our property, but they were a softer cherry with a sour taste when eaten directly from the tree. These cherries were better used for bottling in order to be enjoyed during colder months, or for the making of jelly jam to be used all year long. However, once we became accustomed with the sour taste, we would spend hours high up in the trees munching on the cherries. Climbing higher and higher, reaching out on branches, we discovered how far we could go without breaking a branch or falling. Interestingly, once we had grown up and left home, no longer spending time in the trees picking cherries, birds moved in, so our parents had few cherries to preserve or to make into jelly.

Shortly after moving to the homestead, we also discovered that grape vines grew wildly on the fence that separated the back of our property from the gypsum company property. Despite being annually cut back or burned, these vines would always grow back the following year. The grapes were particularly sour to eat directly off the vine – even more sour than our cherries. So once again, my mother learned to use them to make excellent grape jelly jam. .

There was a large vegetable garden between the grape vines and the back of our barn. Potatoes, carrots, radishes, and beans grew well, but more delicate vegetables grew poorly or not at all. As well, the garden never failed to produce annually a superior crop of rocks. We never discovered from where those rocks came. But we tossed thousands of them into a gully that was directly behind the barn. This gully eventually disappeared after about ten years of being filled by rocks and other debris (including coal ashes and kitchen scraps). Several shingles on the side of the barn would fall off each year due to being hit so frequently by tossed rocks.

The driveway beside the house was relatively flat as was the sidewalk in front of the house. How flat were they? Well, some winters when there was a thaw followed by a quick freeze, we would awake to discover that a skating rink had formed from our back-door along the driveway and down the sidewalk. We still have family home movies of us skating on our own unique rink.

All in all, the location of the homestead had a lot going for it. Of greater appeal than the grounds, however, was the interior design of the house and barn. The house itself was a spacious two-storied building with an unfinished basement under half of the house. The barn was also a large two-storied structure which was typical of residences built in the horse-and-buggy era – sufficient room for the horse, wagon, hay and feed. An enclosed one-storied back room connected the house and barn, with yet two smaller rooms that ran along the sides of the back room. As children, we used one of these smaller rooms as a club room.

For some long-forgotten reason, Laurie and I arrived at the unusual idea to dig an underground tunnel to the outside. Most likely, we had seen a movie in which the actors had dug a tunnel. In any case, it sounded like a great idea at the time.

Laurie: "We can carefully lift up the floor boards of the club room, so we can later replace them. Nobody will see this entrance way to the tunnel."

Stewart: "Okay. We can then dump the dirt in the gully behind the barn. That way, nobody will even notice or detect that we are doing something."

Laurie: "Also, once we get into the tunnel and replace the floor boards, we will be able to fool our brothers, Darrell and Graham, as to how we have disappeared from the room."

Stewart: "Sounds like a great idea. Let's do it."

To our great surprise, however, we discovered a concrete chamber about six to eight feet squared, and about five feet high under the floor boards. It had apparently been a root cellar or cold room for keeping vegetables and bottled preserves. After root cellars had fallen out of common usage, earlier owners of the house had apparently filled-in the chamber with dirt and debris. As we dug out the chamber, we discovered hidden "treasures" like a mousetrap that could catch four mice at one setting (see another short story for details).

However, the concrete walls put an end to our plan to dig a horizontal tunnel to the outside. So, instead, we simply converted the chamber into our new secret club house. We also built a table and chairs to place inside it, and used candles to light the chamber.

If this account of "digging down" sounds to be on the wild side, it was nothing compared to "jumping out" of the barn's second-story windows. Of course, being kids, our bodies were a lot more flexible and could tolerate such leaps. Just the same, we were not completely infallible.

For example, on a previous occasion when we lived in the apartment on Prince Street, at about age six, I seriously broke my left arm at the elbow. While playing with three other kids on a log that rested on a sawhorse pretending it to be a horse, everything tipped over backwards.

My broken elbow was too severe for the hospital in Wolfville, about ten miles away, to handle, so they stabilized me for the night. Next day, our family doctor (Dr. Basheau) stretched me out on the back seat of his car, and he personally drove me and my father to a major hospital in Halifax. There were apparently no ambulances in those days, and certainly no Medicare coverage.

In any case, let's return to leaping from the second floor of a barn. Laurie and I, after due if not thoughtful consideration, came to the conclusion that by hanging by our fingertips from the barn's second-storied window, our feet would be just above the first-floor window. Therefore, we were really only jumping from the first-floor window which in our odd way of thinking was manageable. Fooling ourselves that we were only jumping from the first floor and not the second seemed to work. At least, it made us feel more confident. Besides, nobody had ever broken a bone or suffered other major personal injury by jumping from the first floor – had they?

Perhaps it was perverted thinking, but we made the jump numerous times. Nobody was ever injured, which gave "proof" that our thinking was in fact correct. But to place things in proper perspective, we were much more likely to depart from the barn's second floor by using the staircase at least 99.9% of the time, rather than jumping from the second floor.

It is difficult to identify and calculate the importance of one's home and neighbourhood in terms of how they develop as human beings. Actually, it is beyond calculation. Yes, they are important, that goes without question, but to pinpoint the importance is not manageable. The presence of nearby woodlands, the Prince Street apartment, and the William Street homestead were all essential ingredients as to how I was raised. We spent so much time in these settings, "my home in the 'hood," feeding our appetite for exploration and discovery.

3

SCHOOL DAYS — EVERYTHING BUT EDUCATION

Hantsport is large enough to have neighbourhoods but small enough for everybody to come together. Diversities existed during the 1950s and early 1960s yet we still had a strong sense of common identity. Naturally, we were most familiar with people and patterns of life within our separate neighbourhoods. Yet the town's diversities were knitted together through our one common school and on the sporting fields of play. Of course, this coming together of body and mind also occurred elsewhere in Hantsport. For example, membership in associations like Boy Scouts and Girl Guides or playing on the river front or going to the Saturday matinee at the movie theatre were important in forging a sense of community.

But let us take a closer look at school days. I always liked going to school but not necessarily to acquire new knowledge. Instead, I enjoyed the social comradeship and the pattern of daily regularity that school provided. School was never a prison for me, but a springboard to develop a broader sense of identity with the community. When it comes to what I remember the most about school, it was not textbook material or classroom lessons. It was everything else – the opportunity to associate with so many others, and to share different experiences with others both in classrooms and sporting fields.

a. Early Grades, 1950-1960

Books and stories had always been a major part of my family life as far back as I can remember. In fact, I still possess some of my childhood books on such characters as Roy Rogers, Tarzan, Gene Autry, Lassie, Aladdin and Robin Hood. Such childhood novels as *Wind in the Willows* and *20,000 Leagues under the Sea* are still part of my book collection. My mother and father introduced me and my siblings at an early age to the world of stories which stretched the mind of imagination. My paternal grandfather got me hooked on the disciplined habit of reading, clipping and saving the *"Uncle Ray Corner"* column on historical and social facts that used to appear in the daily newspaper

Reading, writing, and applyting one's imagination, however, are individual activities that can be done anywhere. Going to school, on the other hand, was a social activity; this was the part of education that I really enjoyed. I could handle the reading and homework requirements, sufficient enough to pass courses but without receiving outstanding grades. The preceding statement, however, requires clarification. On the one hand, I did repeat Grade IV. You could say that I enjoyed the grade so much that I decided to take it a second time. Or you could say that I had goofed around too much the first year so that I was forced to repeat the grade. I will leave it to the reader to figure out the correct answer. A second qualification is that after grade school, I was fortunate enough to receive three university degrees including a Ph.D., and then I taught university courses for about 39 years. So I guess that I did learn something at school.

I cannot remember the actual first day that I went to school. But only recall starting kindergarten in the fall of 1950. Ronnie and Lenny, who were slightly older and a grade or two ahead of me and who lived in the same apartment building on Prince Street, took me with them during my first few days in kindergarten.

The school building was about one-and-a-half blocks away. It was just up Prince Street, across Main Street, and a short distance on the right along School Street. A large two-story, wooden building, encircled by a large gravel play area. Some swings and teeter-totters were located out of sight behind the school building, probably because authorities were too embarrassed with the dilapidated equipment. There was no gymnasium, athletic field, or libraries that are the norm with modern schools. Fortunately, there was a small bookstore/reading room, run by Miss Wall, directly opposite the Post Office on William Street that supplied our fix of reading material.

In any case, the walks to school in the morning or after lunch, and the return walks home, were sometimes in the company of Mr. Frank Newcomb. What with his lengthy strides, it was difficult for small kids to keep up with him. Nevertheless, our hearts pounded with pride to be in the presence of this man.

During our first few years of school, Mr. Newcomb in a small child's eyes seemed to run the school. He was not the school principal; and he was not our classroom teacher. Instead, as the school's janitor, Mr. Newcomb seemed to control everything else. He shoveled the snow; fed coal into the school furnace; fixed radiators in each classroom; replaced burned out light bulbs; took out coal ashes to the coal ash pile; and repaired the water fountains and washrooms. Mr. Newcomb was everywhere and he did everything. He was the boss of the school!

Perhaps most importantly, Mr. Newcomb got to know you. We were just five-year olds in kindergarten, yet Mr. Newcomb would talk with you as a person on those walks to and from school. This was the kind of sociability that made school life so inviting in Hantsport.

Kindergarten was extra special. Like other kindergartens in other schools, ours consisted mainly of games, sing-songs, and fun-filled learning activities. In addition, our kindergarten teacher, Miss Lawrence, would take us alternately to the school's buzzer just outside our classroom. There, we could buzz the whole school as to recess time or the end of classes for the day, with all fellow students in every grade waiting for our finger on the buzzer.

In the early grades, I looked forward each day to getting another red, blue, or silver "stick-on" star to be added next to my name on the wall poster for best attendance. Actually, the truth of the matter is that I rarely if ever received an award for highest grade in an academic subject at the end of each class year. But when it came to best attendance record,

I was a shoo-in winner; hence, I was at a complete lost in the higher grades when prizes were no longer given out for best attendance, not even multi-coloured stick-on stars!

The early grades were filled with fun and enjoyment, as we got to know our fellow students from across town. We had song booklets from which we sang songs, like *"Row, Row the Boat"* and *"Frog Went a Courting."* We never seemed to grow tired of these and other favourite songs, as we repeated them grade after grade for several years. It was especially fun when we sang in the round (if that's the correct term), where half of the class sang one line while the other half sang a different line.

Occasionally, films of the National Film Board of Canada were shown in the earlier classes. For example, the award-winning anti-war film, *Neighbours*, had such a long-lasting impact on me, that I often used it many decades later in my university political science courses to spark classroom discussion.

During recess, we played *"King of the Hill"* on the pile of coal ashes. (Yes, we played in an ash pile – now you know how dilapidated those swings and teeter-totters really were.) With this game, we would try to push and pull everybody else off the hill, in order to become the last one standing on the hill. Within a second of being crowned the new "King," everybody else would then seek to replace you. Because he was much larger than the rest of us in our age group, Harry seemed to dominate in being "King." Other times, we would simply run around the graveled school yard playing *"Tag."* I suspect that many of today's over-protective parents would be horrified with the thought of their children rough-housing on a pile of ashes, or running around on gravel scratching their hands and knees. But it is unbelievable the joy we had in doing our own things.

For example, on one occasion during afternoon recess in grade two, we were "high" with excitement. How high? We continued playing tag as we rushed to our seats inside the classroom. I even playfully stuck out my leg as my very best friend, Robin, went past my desk. He did not see my leg but went flying down the aisle. I was stunned in amazement with what I saw. Robin, in his rush and tripping over my foot, was stretched out flying horizontally down the aisle – just like Superman but minus a cape!

The next thing I realized, I was standing next to the teacher's desk. Still stunned with what had just happened. As the teacher scolded me for being a naughty boy, she took out the dreaded leather strap from her desk's top drawer. WHAM! ...WHAM! ... (and for good measure, another WHAM!) Across the palm of the hand, and I had to stand in the corner for the remainder of the class period.

For the most part, we did not mind playing on the ash pile or running around on the stony gravel yard. We did not know what a proper playground was. This was a time before the construction of the playground with a wading pool at the Community Centre a few years later in the mid-1950s. The construction of the wading pool was shortly followed by the construction of a swimming pool and tennis court. We had never seen let alone played in a gymnasium.

Curiously, however, as we discovered in subsequent years, there was a basketball building, outdoor hockey rink, and the town's major baseball field on the other side of School Street. But we never had access to those recreational facilities during school time. Possibly school authorities did not want small kids crossing the street. Or perhaps, the authorities were ignorant as to the importance of physical exercise for a proper education.

As was mentioned earlier, I enjoyed going to school even though my grades were not the best. In Nova Scotia at the time, the early grades ended with grade eight, and high school started with grade nine. My course marks during the early years had been passable, usually in the 50s to 70s range, but my prospects were not great. Eventually in grade eight, I decided that I had better pull up my socks if I wished to realize my dream career goal to become a veterinarian.

b. Later Grades, 1960-1963

High school had always been a major turning point for many students in Nova Scotia. Several students would leave school to get a job. Yet other students could not afford to stay in school because it was necessary to buy your school books at the high-school level. Consequently, grade eight students had to line-up a current grade nine student ahead of time in order to buy cheaply their used books.

By coincidence in 1956, Robert Stanfield led his Progressive Conservative party to victory in a general election in Nova Scotia. Eventually, the Stanfield government implemented its campaign promise for the government to rent all high school books to each student for about $5 per grade. This simple change made high school affordable to all students regardless of family income. Meritocracy became the key factor – a student could and should continue their education if they had the ability and skills to do so. Stanfield's policy also sparked my personal interest – a career changer – as to what could be achieved by government acting thoughtfully to serve the public interest.

Government financing changes certainly made it easier to continue at grade school. But I still had to do something to improve my course marks. I came to the conclusion that I was only scraping by because I was aiming to achieve the passing grade of "50." Even though I was passing my courses, some of my marks were very low. So I decided to aim higher the following year when I entered grade nine, by making "60" my personal passing mark. My individual marks and average went up. Consequently, I repeatedly increased my personal passing bar by another five points in each subsequent year at high school and continued this practice at university. My standing continued to improve each year so that "A" level grades became standard during my Ph.D. studies at university in the early 1970s.

Meanwhile, there was another, most exciting development on the educational front, with the opening of the new school building. Classes were first held in the new school in September 1961; the gymnasium was completed in November of the same year. Then the new school had its official opening on December 11, 1961. Admittedly, the teachers in the new building were mostly the same as in the former school building, as were the fellow students and curriculum. The new school also continued to provide education up to and including grade eleven like the former school. I went to this new school for grade ten, and returned the following year for grade eleven.

The new school building was only across the street from the previous, older school. It was located on property that had been mainly occupied by an outdoor skating arena and a basketball building. Compared to the older building, the new one had cleaner and more spacious rooms. There was also a properly equipped lab for chemistry and physics science courses.

Without question, however, the most exciting feature of the new school building was its attached gymnasium that could be used for basketball, volleyball, and badminton. Of course, like other multi-use gyms, ours was also used for the writing of exams and graduation ceremonies, and for public events like Remembrance Day ceremonies. There were also proper change rooms with shower facilities for both gym athletic activities and outdoor sports. We still did not have proper physical education instructors. Instead, our home room class teachers usually oversaw exercises during class time. It was quite a shock to see some of our teachers, especially Miss Whitman, in sneakers at gym class. In addition, Mr. Allister Clark, the school's principal and teacher of economics, history and some other courses usually volunteered to coach many of the extra-curricular sports played by the boys.

School was not only a matter of passing courses and getting good grades. Nor was it about fun and games, and the occasional instances of corporal punishment. Much of the '50s and early '60s era was centred on its pop music culture. It was eclectic in nature, expressed in diverse musical genres. One such genre was the teenage tragedy (or death) song, like *"Tell Laura I Love Her"* and *"Leader of the Pack."* Unfortunately, this music genre struck home when Bill Hicking, possibly the most popular boy in town, was killed in a car accident in November 1962. The whole school body marched en masse to his funeral held at the Anglican Church. Within a few years, after I had moved on to university, two other long-time friends also perished in separate car accidents. Just as we had shared a common life growing up, the community mourned together when each departed.

c. Grade XII, 1964-1964

The Hantsport school did not offer grade twelve, so it was necessary to go to the regional high school in Windsor, seven miles away, to complete our high school education. Just the same, there were some very good teachers at the Windsor school, and I was taking my studies more seriously because I was planning to start university the following year. Once again, I remember the Windsor school not so much for what we learned in the classroom. Instead, I remember the experiences that came with the daily routine of going to school.

There was a school bus service but, more often than not, the four boys would miss the morning bus so we would hitch hike. (The four girls for some reason always caught the bus.) Since I played on the soccer team in the fall and the basketball team in the winter, I don't ever recall returning home by bus, so it was also necessary to hitch hike home after practice or a game.

Hitch hiking was quite common at that time. We also usually had great luck hitch hiking, never waiting long to catch a ride. Often somebody from Hantsport would recognize us and stop to give us a ride. On other occasions, when strangers picked us up, they were civil for the most part only occasionally being oddballs.

In any case, on one Friday afternoon after a soccer game, on hitch-hiking home, I was picked up by two Roman Catholic priests. They had the car radio on rather loud and, as I got into the back seat, the driver immediately asked if I had heard the news. Of course, I hadn't but neither priest informed me of the pressing news. Nevertheless, the radio soon filled in the gap, as nobody said a word for the remainder of the trip. By the way, that Friday afternoon was Nov. 22, 1963, and President Kennedy of USA had just been shot.

When I arrived home, television stations in North America had joined services to provide coverage of Kennedy's death and related assassination developments. Similar coverage followed the next day on a Saturday when most people were at home. The accused assassin, Lee Harvey Oswald, was in turn murdered by Jack Ruby for all to watch. We had been shocked with Kennedy's assassination, but now were startled with the second murder. We saw in real time a person actually being murdered. This was not a tape, it was not a movie or television program; but it was the real thing. We lost our innocence on those two days – perhaps it was naïve innocence to begin with, but we lost it. We were no longer school children, but mature citizens of the world.

d. On the Playing Fields

Some readers will no doubt link the title of this section to the Duke of Wellington's comment that the battle of Waterloo was won on the "Playing Fields of Eton," and to similar references. (Google again if you wish.) The notion that sports can generate co-operation, cohesiveness, discipline and equality, even in elite educational institutions such as Eton, is appealing. Yet others have likewise stressed the need to train both body and mind.

"Alley Oop ... Oop ... Oop ... Oop," we chanted in unison every time that this baseball opponent from the neighbouring town of Windsor came up to bat. All the way from the dug-out to the batter's box, we repeated the melodic line, "Alley Oop ... Oop ... Oop ... Oop."

We couldn't help ourselves. Not only was *"Alley Oop"* the current novelty hit song, a one-hit wonder, of the summer of 1960. But the target of our attention was lanky in stature, a bit slumped at the shoulders, sloppy in clothing and a bit of a loud-mouthed "yakker" of trash talk. He also dragged his bat on the ground, like a club, as he approached the batting box. He was the splitting image of a caveman like the comic-strip character of the same name as the song, besides, he was from Windsor, so it was okay for us to joke about our neighbourly opponents.

John Paris seemed to be the leader of this Windsor group of players. Although John was good in most sports, he was most notably a talented hockey player. In fact, John was recruited by Scotty Bowman in the spring of 1963 to play junior-level hockey with a team that was part of the Montreal *Canadiens* network of teams. Although John did not make the cut, he returned to the Windsor Regional High School where we played soccer together during the fall of 1963. John eventually made his mark in hockey by becoming the first black professional coach to win his league's championship (Paris 2014).

It was not common yet it was neither unusual for a group of ball players from Windsor, including the Alley Oop look-alike and John, to travel to Hantsport for a game of baseball. In those days, there were no uniforms, no batting helmets, no league and no schedule. I have no idea who arranged these on-the-spot games. Gloves, bats, and balls were often shared between the two teams. It was simply a matter of being the natural thing to do. After all, it was a hot, sunny summer day, with a vacant baseball field. So we said "let's play ball" and we did.

As team-mates, we differed greatly in baseball skills but we all enjoyed playing together. A few of our players (including John Bishop, John Ainsworth, and Laurie Johnson) did advance to play a bit for the *Hantsport Shamrocks* in senior baseball at the provincial level. But most of us were not that talented; instead, baseball was just a way to pass the time. The Windsor players similarly matched our level of mediocrity, and shared our love for the game.

While it was a joy to play against the Windsor players, it was rare because of the distance apart. Thus, most times, we competed amongst ourselves and not with outsiders. There were just enough boys in Hantsport of similar ages to form about three baseball teams, each with about ten or eleven players if everybody showed up. This became the common pattern in Hantsport during the '50s and early '60s. Even at an earlier age, back in our separate neighbourhoods, four or five kids might get together on a patch of grass to play ball. So everybody who wished to play participated regardless of their talent skills. This became the pattern in most sports we played – equality in participation.

The most memorable unorganized event, however, was the annual "Mud Bowl" in football. Usually on a Saturday afternoon right after a hurricane in September, or sometimes in August, kids would gather by instinct at the outfield of the baseball field. The field would be covered with mud-puddles from the storm, and otherwise soft and muddy.

We would naturally divide ourselves into two teams based on which side of Main Street that we lived. Once again, there were no uniforms, no protection, no referees, and no equipment (except for a football). We just played, and rarely got hurt. The main "unwritten rule" was to tackle an opponent in a mud-puddle. In no time at all, we were all unrecognizable as everybody was drenched wet and covered in mud. Nobody kept track of the score. We were just out to have fun. If one team seemed to be overly dominant, then players would reshuffle themselves to even-up the teams. At the Mud Ball of 1960, we had a luxury – a post-game shower. Construction workers at the new school building had left a water hose at the site. So we were able to turn it on to wash ourselves and then actually see with certainty who was on each team.

Ad hoc sporting activities remained common. Increasingly, however, with the construction of the swimming pool and school gymnasium, sports took on a more organized direction. Coaches and uniforms were introduced, and teams began to represent the town more vigorously at competitions. Whatever the format, the playing fields taught us lessons of leadership and teamwork, and, above all, the value of respect for others.

BETWEEN NOSTALGIA AND A BRAVE NEW WORLD

Mention has already been made and will be made again that Hantsport during the 1950s and early 1960s was in a state of transition. No doubt, this observation is also valid with other communities at the same time – it was one of those turning-point occasions in history. There were still traditional ways of living and doing things, so familiar and deeply embedded, that had arisen mostly in the pre-war and wartime years. Yet at the same time, technological and other changes were rapidly unfolding during the post-war era. We were strongly attached to the tried, true and familiar, for which we had strong feelings of nostalgia. But at the same time, we were attracted by the promise for a better future – a brave new world – promised by the advent of television, the Sputnik Decade (1957-67) and similar developments. It was a most invigorating time in which to live.

a. Feelings of Nostalgia

Perhaps the earliest of my memories are associated with the L. B. Harvie grocery store. Located on William Street at the bottom of Oak Street, Harvie's was one of Hantsport's three main grocery stores at that time. Since Harvie's was closest to my home, it was the most familiar to me.

No doubt I started going to Harvie's with my mother in the very late 1940s for what became almost daily visits.

As a very young child, I noticed the structure of the store, its people, and most importantly how it operated. Everybody knew everybody else by first name. Staff knew their customers, and customers knew the staff, including Mr. L. B. Harvie. The store provided a truly personalized, hands-on service. Harvie's was not just a corner grocery store, but it was the corner-stone of the local neighbourhood.

One of the most fascinating features of Harvie's was its very high ceiling (in the eyes of small children), with grocery items stocked along the walls up to the ceiling. This was in stark contrast to the design of modern (early 21st century) grocery stores and supermarkets, where customers are required to go up and down aisles, usually with a shopping cart, to pick up their own groceries But at Harvie's, only store clerks had access to the grocery items.

A customer would give a shopping list to a clerk; the clerk would then go through the store to pick up the items. Each clerk used a "reacher" (it may have had a different technical name) to grab a can of soup or box of cereal at ceiling level. The "reacher" was a long wooden pole with a metal attachment for a handle at one end and a grabbing device at the other end. By manipulating the handle, the clerk could open and close the grabbing device. This was real entertainment in the eyes of kids, and no doubt many adults as well. Each store clerk would expertly manipulate this open-and-release mechanism to reach the most unreachable items.

The clerk's work, however, would not be completed with collecting the grocery items. Harvie's existed at a time when groceries were sold on the basis of credit to be paid at the end of the month. So after collecting the items, the clerk would carefully go over the customer's shopping list to make certain that each item had in fact been collected. The items would then be recorded by hand with their respective prices on the customer's charge account. The customer would pay the total accumulated bill, or a portion of it, at the end of the month or later. For large orders, home delivery was available by horse and wagon before being replaced by a station wagon or truck.

Usually parents would do the major grocery shopping once per week; and overlooked items would be picked up during the week. Sometimes mothers would send a child to pick up one or a few items at Harvie's. When we lived on Prince Street, I would run through a patch of woods (where the fire station is now located) within a minute or two to Harvie's. The store clerks, who knew me, would automatically accept my grocery request, and charge the item to the family's monthly bill.

To watch the clerks maneuver their pole reachers was fascinating. But there were other delights in the back portion of the Harvie store where the meat department was located. The store was renowned for its meats with Mr. L. B. Harvie being the butcher; his son, John, also worked there as a butcher. What appeared to kids to be a very large, waist-high tree stump, served as a cutting block. The floor appeared to be covered with sawdust or wood shavings. Meats were sawed, chopped and sliced to meet the customer's specific request; then the portions were individually wrapped in brownish, wax-coated paper and tied with a string.

Both mister Harvies were always open and friendly, with time for a kind chat with each of the neighbourhood kids. Just as importantly, both went out of the way to fulfill freely our special requests – what requests could kids have in a grocery store?

Needed a cardboard box, and what kid did not have "1001" reasons for boxes? They were free for the taking. Often, in addition, wooden orange or fruit crates were available. These crates were particularly valuable because they had so many different uses, or the wood could be re-used to build things. I learned early to place a crate on one end to be a bedside table, with a lamp placed on top of the other end. Inside, I kept my bedtime book on the middle shelve and toys in the bottom part of the crate.

And where there's meat, there are bones! As kids, we never had any hesitancy to approach misters L. B. and John Harvie, and ask if they had a bone for our dog. But you had to be careful for what you asked, as my sister once learned.

Pam asked, "Do you have any dog bones?"

Mr. John Harvie replied with his distinctive drawl (like James Stewart, the movie actor), "No, we do not have any dog bones." This response left my sister momentarily stunned and speechless because bones for our dog had always been available previously.

But Mr. Harvie continued his response with this clarification, "But we do have bones for dogs."

My sister learned from this subtle difference in phrasing, and would always request in the future "a bone for my dog" and not "a dog bone."

These fond memories of Harvie's came to an abrupt end one night, sometime in the early- to mid-fifties (possibly 1953) when the store burned to the ground. If my memory is correct, some kid playing with matches was the arsonist. The store was rebuilt but eventually fell victim to the coincidental growth of grocery chains and supermarkets. Independent grocery stores like Harvie's, despite their unique and personalized service, could not compete with these new players in the grocery business.

A second favourite store from the very late 1940s and very early 1950s was the drug store. The Rexall drug store was run by Mr. R. W. Zinck, the pharmacist. It was located on Main Street, near the corner of Prince Street. But the Zinck drug store was on the opposite side of Main Street compared to the current (2017) drug store. Next to the Zinck drug store was a gas station and garage, which is now the location of the liquor store.

It might sound strange to mention a drug store as being a child's favourite store. But just as Harvie's was an attraction because of its reaching poles, cardboard and wooden boxes, and bones for dogs, the drug store was attractive to children because of its non-drug features. It had an ice cream and milkshake counter!

Whenever my mother took me uptown on a shopping trip, we would often stop for an ice cream treat. Also the seats at the ice cream counter were round stools, and we could playfully spin around endlessly on those stools. This was part of a bygone era when many drug stores commonly had an ice cream counter. Today, we only see drug store ice cream counters in old black and white movies from the 1930s and

1940s. Zinck's eventually got rid of its ice cream counter and stools, which became a faded memory of the past.

"First memories" are often difficult to identify as such. Oftentimes, first memories are those of your parents or other close relatives who constantly remind you of earlier experiences. There is so much repetition that their memories also become your memories.

I can say with confidence, however, that one of my actual first memories was the coming of the ice man. This was in the very early 1950s when we lived in an apartment on Prince Street, opposite to the intersection with Porter's Avenue. Our apartment unit was half of the top floor of a two-story building. We had an icebox like most other families, not a refrigerator. Inside the icebox, there was a compartment for a large block of ice to keep food cold; and a pan would catch water from the ice as it slowly melted. Water would still frequently spill over the pan's side edges inside the icebox, or as the pan was carried to the kitchen sink to be emptied.

On a hot summer day, when the ice man came on his weekly route to deliver new blocks of ice, kids would gather around his truck. The ice blocks were apparently cut from frozen lake water each winter. Then they were covered by sawdust and a large canvass tarpaulin to retard the ice from melting, and delivered by truck all year long to individual homes.

When the ice man used his steel clamps to carry a block of ice into a home, kids would jump into action. The floor of the truck would be covered with chunks of chipped ice. We would each grab a hand-sized chunk, brush off the sawdust and spend the next while sucking and chomping the chunk of ice. It was not a flavoured *Popsicle*. But it was the next best thing, fresh frozen lake water from the previous winter, and it was free.

The slopping and spilling of water from the melting ice block was a major household problem. If this was not "writing on the wall" of the icebox's demise, its failure to keep food freezing cold did signal its end. Yes, the icebox worked fine with food that had to be kept cool. But there was no equivalent success with food that had to be kept cold or freezing cold like ice cream. Once refrigerators became affordable, families made the immediate switch away from the icebox. The ice man thus quickly disappeared from the scene, frozen in time past.

My memories of Harvie's, Zinck's and the ice man were when they were still present but then disappeared from the scene. However, when it comes to horses and wagons, they were already a rarity. They were seldom seen in town, relics from a bygone era. The vast majority of people by the late 1940s and early 1950s had cars or trucks. Within and about town, people walked or used bicycles a lot more than is the case today. Nevertheless, at least two of the three grocery stores still used horse and wagon to deliver groceries, but these were soon replaced with motorized vehicles.

There was, however, one man from the near-by community of Bishopville or thereabout who would come into Hantsport from time to time with his horse and wagon. Unfortunately, I do not think I ever knew his name. But what a treat it was to see him! On his return trip home usually in the late afternoon, he would head up Holmes Hill. He allowed us to jump onto the back of his wagon for a ride. It was a thrill to hear the horse slowly but steadily clopping, clopping along. The tell-tailed odour from freshly dropped horse manure or horse fart surrounded us. We loved it! To see the massive rippling muscle power of the horse under the man's reins control was marvelous. When we reached the three-street intersection at the top end of Holmes Hill, we would jump off the wagon, politely thank the kind man for the ride, wave a good-bye and begin our long walk home in time for supper.

b. A Brave New World?

There was more than a bit of nostalgia felt with the disappearance of the old-style Harvie grocery store, Zinck's ice cream counter, and the ice man. But with many other seemingly minor changes, there were only feelings of acceptance or inevitability. For example, we were aware that to see a horse and wagon in town, albeit a thrill, was really a glimpse of the past.

At the same time, the long-termed impact of some other changes was not immediately obvious. For example, for many years, Hantsport's

Main Street was part of Nova Scotia's highway #1. This was actually true throughout the Annapolis Valley. Each town's main street, regardless of its specific street name, was part of highway #1. This had been the case for decades. Apparently, in order to reduce drive-through traffic on Main Street, highway #1 was re-routed onto Willow Street in the early 1950s. However, buses continued to use Main Street for several years, stopping at the Oldershaw grocery store at the corner of Main and Prince Streets (the present location of the town hall). Later, with the construction of highway #101 that by-passes Hantsport and other Valley communities, buses and most other traffic stopped completely coming into town. Today, the town's few remaining business owners and politicians constantly bemoan the weak customer numbers and ponder how to re-attract traffic and increase their customer base. Go figure.

There was yet another change that was not confined to Hantsport. The Dominion Atlantic Railroad, like other railroads, switched in the early 1950s from its black steam-driven engines that used coal to diesel fueled engines. There was some feeling of nostalgia admittedly expressed at the time for the passing of the steam engine. Those large, black steam engines always seemed to be like gigantic living beasts with their moving parts visible for all to see and their sudden hissing release of clouds of white steam. The sudden and irregular release of that steam would never fail to scare the "B'Jesus" out of us, but we still enjoyed the thrill of it all.

But the change to diesel was generally considered to be necessary for the rail business to remain competitive. Nevertheless, the passenger train service continued to decline steadily during the late years of the 20th century, as did the freight trains. Although the gypsum ore trains lasted for many more additional years, they also stopped running with change in the industrial market for gypsum during the early 21st century.

There was yet a third set of changes that did not stir feelings of nostalgia or of inevitable acceptance. Instead, these changes were large in scope and obvious in terms of potential impact. Construction of the outdoor swimming pool in 1955, the replacement of the old school in 1961 and the arrival of television during the early 1950s were greeted with excitement and high expectations. We were definitely entering a brave new world – only time would reveal the truth.

Despite years of trying, I had never learned to swim when swimming lessons used to be held on the beach. But the construction of the new outdoor pool at the Community Centre was a major and most welcomed change for the community. It had proper changing rooms with showers; in fact, my father had done the plumbing and installed the pipes for the pool and change facilities. Was he the first to ever swim, albeit unofficially, in the pool? Better qualified staff was also hired to teach both children and adults how to swim. The claim that the pool was the best outdoor pool east of Montreal was somewhat misleading. After all, I could never understand the wisdom of an outdoor swimming pool in a location whose climate restricted the pool's use to only two months per year (July and August).

Although like numerous others I finally learned to swim in the new pool, I never became a competitive or great swimmer. Following a fracture of my left elbow in the early 1950s, my arm was noticeably crooked so I would always go to my right when I swam. I suppose that if swimming lanes were circular like a horse race track and swimming was in a counter-clockwise direction, I could have become an internationally ranked swimmer.

Located on School Street, the old school was the second building on the right from the intersection with Main Street. This building had two stories of classrooms, one per grade. Plus there were extra spaces in the basement (home economics for the girls and carpentry for the boys). This old school building seemed to have been around for ages, although it had been expanded or renovated at different times over the years. Actually, portions of the old school had apparently been around for over 100 years. There were a few rickety old swings and teeter-totters in the back of the old school. But most students played by running around the gravel yard that encircled the building, or by just walking and talking. There was no formal physical education, and very few sport activities. Personally, I went to school in this building from kindergarten up to, and including, grade nine. But I doubt if anybody was sad to leave in favour of the new school building.

35

In addition to the new school, the Nova Scotia government by coincidence introduced the use of television for a couple of courses. But this innovation proved disappointing. As the first television generation, we had been watching television for several years by this time, and were well aware of the exciting entertainment programs on television. We had been watching Elvis Presley and other popular entertainers gyrate on the *Ed Sullivan Show* since the mid-fifties, and now we had to listen to this stiff lecture about the niceties of math formulae. No competition: "A" for good intentions, but an "F" for performance.

However, the most sweeping or transformative change experienced at the time was the advent of television. Even though initial television viewers in Hantsport only had access to one channel and it was on air for only a few hours each evening, the range of televised programs was such that the local movie theatre could not compete. As well, picture quality was usually grainy, yet people stayed at home religiously to watch their favourite programs. Much can be written and has been written about the introduction of television in the early- to mid-fifties, but let's focus on one element: its "believability."

Possibly the public was overwhelmed by the addictive impact of rapidly moving pictures; by the presence of the television set in our living-room; or by the large number of "live" performances in the early days of television. Personally, I was really taken in by the program, *You Are There*. Not only was the program hosted by one of the USA's most respected journalists (Walter Cronkite), it was sponsored by *Mutual of Omaha* (*Prudential*), an insurance company with the Rock of Gibraltar as its symbol.. Each week, my impression was that through the "magic" of television, Cronkite would actually go back across time, via a time machine, to interview famous people like Joanne d'Arc. Such was the believability element in the early days of television. Incidents of "payola" and the development of investigative journalism led to a more sophisticated viewership by the sixties and seventies.

The era of the '50s and early '60s was thus a most interesting time in which to live. Charles Dickens is famous for the opening line of his novel, *A Tale of Two Cities*: "it was the best of times, it was

36

the worst of times," so I will not use that line. Instead, I opened this story and followed through with the two-part theme of comfortable familiarity and a brave new world. The era provided a comfortable sense of familiarity and stability that nurtured and fostered our development. Yet, in other matters, changes were occurring that excited us and spurred us to search and work for improvement.

5

FROM THE BIG SCREEN TO THE SMALLER ONE

"**C**hange" is the operative word that characterizes much of the 1950s and early '60s – in fact, there were numerous changes – major changes – in technologies, activities, life style and social values. Hantsport's residents were never at a standstill, but then I suspect that the same was true for much of Canada and other developed countries at that time. Nevertheless, it is an aimless, and endless, debate as to whether the changes we experienced were more significant than those of other eras. That sort of debate is best left to a late night lubricated discussion at the local tavern.

Thus we will focus on the one change that seemed to occur with the blink of an eye both literally and figuratively speaking. Actually, the arrival of television was not just sudden, but, more importantly, it led to the demise of the local movie theatre and children's way of life centred on the Saturday afternoon matinee.

a. Movie Theatre

Saturday afternoons were always special because the movie theatre would have a matinee showing. The featured movie was usually a rip-roaring cowboy/western; or a comedy like *Ma and Pa Kettle*, *Francis the Talking Mule*, the *Three Stooges*, *Abbott and Costello*, or the *Marx*

Brothers. On other occasions, an adventure movie like *Tarzan* or about pirates would be the central feature. Still yet, a mystery or war movie or a suspense drama of broad appeal would be occasionally shown.

These main features were not necessarily recent productions. But we did not care. We were not aware of such things as production dates or latest releases. The movies had to have high entertainment value, and that was all that matter.

Neither were these movies always on top of a film critic's list of recommended movies. Once again, we did not care, because we had no knowledge of the presence of film critics. Rather, we only took into consideration our own rating system of "laughs per minute" and "lingering sense of suspense." Or how bugged-eye we were when we exited the theatre.

Each Saturday matinee movie would usually be preceded by a cartoon. Some of these cartoons, like the *Singing Frog* cartoon, proved to be a classic which we would long remember and talk about. If there was no cartoon, a brief serial like *Lash LaRue* would be shown. The serial episode would always end by leaving us with a cliffhanger of a situation that would not be solved until the following week's episode. So we had no alternative but to show up next week regardless of the featured movie.

The theatre manager/projectionist apparently had a hankering for magic, or feats of illusion. For instance, when the *Houdini* movie (starring Tony Curtis) was shown in the late fifties, I remember that the projectionist came onto the stage to perform some magic tricks to our amazement. Even though his tricks were relatively simple in the world of magic, we were most impressed. After his performance, the manager then proceeded to the projection room to show the movie.

Occasionally, during the week, the projectionist would be present getting the theatre set up for the next showing. He would invite us into the projection room to show us how everything worked. It was all quite revealing and fascinating to get this insider's look. But as kids, we remained more than a bit mystified by the complexity of the equipment and the procedure for projecting films.

The movie theatre was conveniently located opposite to the intersection of William and Oak streets. It was bounded by the railroad track at one end and next to the William Street railroad crossing. Across William Street opposite the theatre, there were the town hall, fire station, Cozy Corner restaurant, Harvie's grocery store, and Dowe's convenience store. The area was a real hive of activity at that time.

With its large seating capacity, the theatre was also used for other community events. School graduation ceremonies were sometimes held here. So were talent contests (like old-time vaudeville shows) where the town's people displayed their musical and other entertainment talents. It was a real eye-opener to see the hidden talent of Tim and other friends or to see otherwise dignified adults let loose on the stage.

In any case, on Saturday afternoons, prior to the opening of the theatre's door, the gravel parking lot outside the theatre was filled with a long line-up of kids. We came together from all across town. Attracted by the magic of movies, we chatted about our favourite actors, the previous week's movie, and the promise of the trailers for this week's movie. And we speculated about what would happen in the next serial episode.

"I don't know how Lash LaRue will escape from the bad guy gunslinger."

"Oh, he will do what he always does, use his bull whip."

"Don't be silly. The gunslinger has two six-shooters. If he's lucky, Lash LaRue can only get one gun with his whip. Then the bad guy will use his other gun to shoot LaRue. Besides, a bullet is faster than the snap of a bull whip."

"I don't know why Lash LaRue is dressed all in black. Don't good guys dress in white hats, and bad guys in black? Gene Autry, the Lone Ranger and Roy Rogers always wear white hats."

"Not always. Sometimes a good guy wears a black hat, like Hopalong Cassidy or Paladin in *Have Gun, Will Travel*. In fact, they dress completely in black"

"Yeah, and then there is the Lone Ranger who wears a white hat plus a black mask over his eyes. He is a good guy with a white hat but why does he wear a mask like a bad guy? I don't get it"

Other times, the on-going conversation turned to the individual actors. Who was the favourite Marx brother, Groucho, Chico, or Harpo? Or the favourite stooge, Larry, Curly, or Moe? Or the better actor in jungle movies: Tarzan, played by Johnny Weissmuller, or Bomba, played by Johnny Sheffield?

"My favourite cowboy actor is Randolph Scott."

"Why? Because he is rough and tough, or is a good guy?"

"No, but I think he lives in Hantsport. There, across the street at Harvie's right now, isn't the man shoveling snow Randolph Scott?"

"Don't be silly. Cowboy actors live and work in Hollywood where they make these movies. That snow shoveler works for the town; he only looks slightly like the movie actor."

"Yeah, movie actors earn tons of money making movies; they don't have to work shoveling snow."

On other occasions, the conversation would turn to political nationalism in respect to the playing of anthems. *"O Canada"* was always played at the start of a showing at the Hantsport theatre, while *"God Save the Queen"* was played at the end. Both renditions required everybody to stand motionless at attention during the playing. Many if not most kids favoured the former anthem but disliked the latter one. So as we stood in the line-up, discussion turned to how to avoid *"God Save the* Queen."

"I don't like having to stand at attention for the anthems. Why can't the manager just show the movies, and forget about the anthems?"

"I don't mind *'O Canada'* because it's Canada's anthem. But the Queen anthem is British, not Canadian."

"Well, the easiest solution is to avoid *'God Save the Queen.'*"

"But how can we do that?"

"Well, the projectionist only starts to play the music after the showing of the production credits. So as the credits start to roll across the screen and before the house lights are turned on, rush for the exit doors, not at the end of the credits."

"I tried that last week but the credit roll was too brief; also, the crowd rushing to the exit was too large. So I was still in the theatre when *'God Save the Queen'* started."

"Yeah, me too. I was out in the lobby standing next to the candy counter, and had to stand at attention with the playing of that British Queen song."

"Why? The lobby is not the theatre. You only have to stand at attention inside the theatre."

"No, the lobby is part of the theatre. After all, you purchase your ticket there."

On and on our conversations went, about everything and nothing. From across town we came to wait patiently in line for the theatre doors to open. We were really taken in by the lure of movies at these Saturday matinees, and equally enjoyed sharing our thoughts. Nothing escaped our attention, the cartoons, serials, major features, favourite actors, selection of candy, playing of anthems and operation of the projection machines. This Saturday afternoon ritual was so firmly fixed that it is still difficult to believe that it would be gone by the late 1950s following the advent of television. But then our conversation quickly shifted to the star appearances on the *Ed Sullivan Show* and other television programs. The newer medium, however, was never as absorbing as the Saturday matinees.

b. Arrival of Television

It is still an eye-opener to reflect back as to the impact that the advent of television had on our generation. Even though initially we only had access to one station, and those old roof-top antennae seemed to deliver only snowy and grainy reception. If my memory is correct, for some unknown reason, my family was the third in town to purchase a television set (around the mid-fifties).

The town's electrician and owner of an electrical appliances store, Mr. David Freeman, was naturally the first to have television. I believe that my father had seen television in the United States when he had briefly worked on the gypsum ships. So he was hooked on this new technology. The fact that he and Mr. Freeman were best friends also counted for something.

Then within a few months, roof-top antennae sprouted like mushrooms as many more residents across town purchased television service. The trickiest task was to align the antenna with the television station in Moncton, New Brunswick (the station's call letters were CKCW). In terms of physical distance, the Hantsport area was physically closer to Halifax, Nova Scotia. But the hilly and rocky terrain that ran down the spine of the province between Halifax and the Annapolis Valley allowed only extremely poor reception of the Halifax station. So by carefully aligning the antenna with the Avon River, Mina Basin, and Bay of Fundy, we had a mainly flat, unobstructed connection with Moncton that provided better but not perfect reception.

What was really interesting, however, with the benefit of hindsight, was how the pattern of daily life changed with a blink of the eye. It all started on the very day that television was installed at my home. At about 5 P. M., there was a knock at the door, and then repeated knocks for the next half-hour or so. This was very unusual because practically everybody in town ate their suppers at that very same time. In any case, it turned out that neighbourhood kids came by to ask if they could come in, to watch television. By the way, it must be kept in mind that in the early days of broadcasting, stations only started to broadcast late in the afternoon around suppertime.

Along with my siblings, on that first evening, we asked our parents for permission to eat supper in the living room while watching television. Thus, the practice of eating family meals together ended. Curiously, our acquisition of television also made it easier for my parents to get baby-sitters, who loved to come because they could watch television when the little-ones had gone to bed.

The *Wild Bill Hickok* western (starring Guy Madison) was the very first television show that I ever saw. *Howdy Doody*, the puppet show, was another early favourite. We soon discovered that there was a standard weekly schedule. Each program would be shown on the same day and time each week; thus, a daily viewing pattern emerged for each day of the week. *Roy Rogers* and other westerns, children programs, as well as comedies like *I Love Lucy* and *Red Skelton,* drama like *Dragnet* and music shows like *Juliette* were also regular favourites. For sporting enthusiasts, the World Series of baseball was shown in the afternoon each and every fall, football games on the weekends, and *Hockey Night in Canada* on Saturday evenings. Local programming like *Don Messer* and *Sing-along Jubilee also* became fixtures, *Walt Disney* on Sunday evenings and *Ed Sullivan* on Sunday nights could not – must not – be overlooked. *Maple Leaf Wrestling* on Friday nights was also a favourite for certain fans. On and on, this list could go as each program had its "own" viewing day and timeslot, year after year.

It is well worthwhile to reconsider the preceding list of television programs. The true significance of the list, while keeping in mind that this particular list was only the proverbial tip of the iceberg, is not the naming of the programs as a memory-recall exercise. Rather it should be recognized that all of the programs were designed to entertain. They were thus in strong competition with the movie theatre business. Instead of having to wait for the arrival of your favourite movie genre to arrive at the local theatre perhaps once or twice per month, there would be a comparable television program at least every week if not more frequently. Furthermore, the television version was available for free and in your own living-room.

Television, however, was never absolutely about entertainment. There was always a place – admittedly a small place in the early years – for news and public affairs programming. But it was not until the 1960s with the development of investigative journalism, that television met its potential. *This Hour Has Seven Days* had a short run but it pioneered the path of investigative journalism in Canada, stimulating the audience rather than force feeding it with zany comedies and corny, fictional presentations.

Many movie theatres, including Hantsport's, could not meet the challenge of the new medium. Perhaps more importantly, however, the long-held habit of children coming together from across town to be amongst themselves to share the viewing of the Saturday afternoon matinee came to an end. We were instead staying at home isolated from each other. Was this the first step in the emergence of the "global village," and supportive evidence of "the medium is the message"

44

with even broader implications? (Readers may google the Internet for Marshall McLuhan's use of these rather complex phrasings).

As children, we never knew what was going on, or why, in the tug-of-war between movie theatres versus television. We only responded like lab rats to the technological media change unfolding before our very eyes. It is only possible today (2017) to look back with the benefit of hindsight at the shift from the big screen to the smaller one, and to speculate about the consequences. Actually, today, instead of being polar opposites, movies and television co-exist as large communication conglomerates.

TREATS AND TRICKS – HALLOWEEN, HANTSPORT STYLE

I n complete stillness, under the moon- and star-lit black sky with an autumn coldness in the air, we stretched out flat, face-down in the tall grass. We had failed in our mission to knock out the light at the top of the tall light-post. Not for lack of trying, for we had tried – sharpening our aim with each toss, using smaller rocks to be more accurate, or larger rocks to get a bigger flash and boom if we should make a hit. Yes, we had tried every trick in our thirteen and fourteen year-old repertoire but had failed to hit the light. But we had attracted attention.

Either a neighbour had squealed upon us, or the police had arrived by chance on their regular, annual Halloween patrol. The beam of the police flashlight crossed above us but was unable to detect our motionless bodies. Was it one of the temporary police officers hired for this, our special night, or was it Chief Allard himself?

"Don't move; whoever it is, they will soon go."

"Yeah, they can only see us when we stand up and can easily be seen in contrast to the flat field."

"But we didn't do a thing. We didn't hit or smash the street lights. So, why should the police be here?"

"Be quiet, don't say a word. "Don't move and don't talk, or they will focus the flashlight in the direction of our voices."

We all thought in mental unison, "stretch out flat and stay still, hug the ground."

How did we ever get into this fix? The evening had started innocently enough just like any other Halloween Eve. Victor had arrived at my family backdoor around supper-time, asking "should we go out to collect treats as in past years, or are we getting to be too old?"

Obviously, we would go, so why ask? The promise of those free tasty treats was too tempting. Besides, with our masks and costumes, nobody would be able to identify us let alone see that we were fourteen year-olds. But, what will we wear?

Halloween in Hantsport (and probably throughout the rest of the province) during the '50s and early '60s was a much simpler affair than today. Now, in the early 21st century, Halloween seems to have become a big commercial occasion with expensive store-bought costumes, make-up, masks, and other decorations. It is also somewhat artificial as parents organize parties for their kids and even chaperon the parties, allegedly to safe-guard children from tampered treats or other harm exaggerated by urban legends. But kids in the '50s and early '60s were on their own to choose and decide how to celebrate the night of the dead.

The first inkling that Halloween was approaching for another year had actually occurred about two or three months earlier. One of the breakfast cereal makers, possibly Kellogg's or Post, would include a full-sized (cardboard) Halloween mask on the back of each carton of cereal. After eating the cereal and emptying the carton, kids would cut out the mask, punch two holes in the marked spots near the mask's ears, tie a string through the two holes, and finally cut out the eye, nose, and mouth slots. That was it. The mask was ready for wearing. Of course, if a kid had the money, a cheap plastic mask could be purchased at the town's "5¢ to $1" department store.

Despite this initial hint that Halloween was approaching, we rarely paid attention to preparing for Halloween night. It was not until 1962 that *"Monster Mash"* appeared as a popular novelty song, sung by Bobbie "Boris" Pickett, when it topped the music charts as an overnight hit. The song is still so popular, at least seasonally popular, that it is played several times per day on radio stations during the week leading up to Halloween. It may also be easily be found online for those who do not wish to wait for the annual playing of the song. In any case, to return to the late 1950s, Halloween still seemed to spring upon us unexpectedly out of the dark. How and why Victor ever kept track of the event, I will never know.

Although we had the masks, what would we do for costumes? More often than not, we would pull on my father's old jackets. Their large size on our small bodies gave a baggy look. Hopefully, if not scary, the jackets were at least sloppy enough for Halloween as we dressed as "tramps." Well, it may not have been all that showy and it certainly was not imaginative, but it got us out of the house to go from door to door in search of treats.

The route that we took was usually the same each year through the familiar local neighbourhood. My family home was on William Street, half-way between Davison Street and the railroad tracks which were about 75 metres away. So zigzagging back-and-forth across the street, we advanced toward the tracks, and then onto Oak, Prince, Davison and again on William streets as well as a side trip up Porter's Avenue. We would hit each and every home. It was our neighbourhood after all and we knew all of the residences like the back of our hand. Nothing escaped our search for treats. Nobody could guess our identity except for Mrs. Bishop. She got us each and every year without exception! How did she do it? It was a short route through the neighbourhood, probably only about thirty to forty homes, but we would be finished by 7 PM or 8 PM, loaded with goodies.

So much for the "treat" part of Halloween, now was the time for the "tricks"!

No doubt, at different times and places, each generation of kids has had their own assortment of favourite tricks. My father used to tell us how in the 1920s and 1930s, in a more rural setting in Bridgetown, he and his older brother annually would tip over a farmer's outhouse.

48

It was always great fun until one year when the farmer let loose a shot of buckshot. This startled the brothers so much that one fell into the pit underneath the tipped-over outhouse. By the '50s, however, I am not aware of anybody in Hantsport who still possessed and used an outhouse, so we never engaged in the art of tipping over outhouses.

For the most part, I suppose that our tricks were tame in comparison. Ours were harmless pranks without evil intent and were not meant to cause harm, at least not to individuals we knew (and we personally knew most of our targets). Of course, on occasion, a prank could go wrong but such occasions were rarities.

With the benefit of hindsight, the most notorious Halloween event that went wrong in the town's history was probably that of 1903. According to David Pollard's book (2010, pp. 115-117), a fifteen year-old by the name of Percy Corkum was shot dead. He was apparently throwing cabbages and turnips against house doors near the last house on Main Street next to the Willow Creek Bridge when shot. Strangely, however, for such a significant, unfortunate event to have occurred in the past, I don't recall any of us in the'50s and '60s ever mentioning it. The event was not even a lasting Halloween "urban legend" in the community's collective memory.

As mentioned above, after collecting our treats, we would next turn our attention to tricks for the remainder of the night. Although Victor would usually drift home to enjoy his treats, the rest of us would meet near the corner of Prince and Oak streets at about 8 PM, coming together from our separate treat gathering runs. Wray, Laurie, Michael, Johnnie, Bobby, Lenny, David, Bill, and I were the usual suspects, when usually five or six of us would meet at about the same time. Never a mean or outrageous group, we were simply out to have a good time by committing pranks.

Somebody would always bring a roll of toilet paper to stretch across the street for the next car that came along to be harmlessly entangled. Others would have cakes of soap to smudge the windshields of parked cars or store windows. Most of us also had firecrackers to be aimlessly set off as we walked along.

Pieces of lawn furniture that had been thoughtlessly left outdoors by careless house-owners were tipped over upside down, while bicycles were hidden behind nearby shrubs. Good nature fun, no willful damage, as we proceeded up Prince Street, then left along Main Street, and finally up Holmes Hill. Members of the gang would sometimes wander off to join other gangs, while in turn other individuals (Wayne, Freddie, Jackie, Jan, Peter, Brian, Walter, Danny, George, and Bruce) would join our group. You went where there was the most fun, or at least where there was the most promise of fun to be had.

On top of Holmes Hill, we were at the edge of the town as the pavement ended to be continued as the dirt road known as the Bog Road. This road should not be confused with the equally appropriately named Bluff Road on the opposite side of town in Kings County in a community called Hants Border. The original cartographers were certainly accurate with their choices of street names, but were never overly imaginative.

Meanwhile, at the juncture of Holmes Hill and the Bog Road, at a 90-degree right angle, there was a third road (Rand Street). Of course, over many years, the terrain, buildings, and use of the area around this "three-street" junction have changed. By the late '50s and early '60s, there was a large field with a tall light post for a street light. This was a favourite stop on Halloween Eve as we tried to knock out the light with stones. We were at this spot when the police arrived.

Our response was to stretch out flat on the ground, to remain motionless in the tall grass, and to remain silent so as not to attract attention. As Michael reminded us, back during the Second World War, "they used to say, 'loose lips can sink ships'." We weren't certain what he was talking about, but we knew better to question Michael's knowledge of the military. Nevertheless, the essence of the message was to remain still, flat, and quiet and that certainly made great sense, which we followed until the police drove away.

With the coast now cleared, we resumed trying to hit the street light. But we had the same degree of success: nil, nada, no luck at all! The fun of the effort soon wore off, especially now that the police had also given up with us being serious trouble-makers. So we moved along to Main Street.

Rather than retrace our steps down Holmes Hill, we pursued ahead on Rand Street, down Riverview Road and School Street, resuming our prank-making activities along the way. Then at the intersection of Prince/School and Main streets, we turned left into the core business section of Main Street. Who should we meet but Geoff, sitting astride his bicycle, the town's major rabble rouser? Only now, Geoff was in charge of Main Street, and he quickly set the ground rules, "Alright, you guys, there will be no destructive activities on my watch, so quiet down and behave yourselves."

"You've got to be kidding," replied Wayne, "are you working for the police?"

"Well," explained Geoff, "Chief Allard can't be everywhere; neither can Fire Chief Harold Warner and the other firefighters who are on duty elsewhere as temporary police officers tonight. So, they hired me to be present on Main Street until 10 PM. But, you shouldn't worry, once my shift is over, I will have my share of fun."

While speaking, Geoff stealthily opened his jacket revealing his stash of three-inch firecrackers compared to our puny one-inchers.

Invariably, Main Street was also where we met our friends from Hants Border. One of the peculiarities of Hantsport is that it is literally on the edge of the boundary between Hants and Kings Counties. One step takes you from Hants County into Kings County, specifically into a community called Hants Border. In fact, Hantsport's Main Street becomes the main street of Hants Border. People in Hants Border usually banked, shopped, worked, and went to church in Hantsport, and otherwise associated in every way with Hantsport's residents. But they did not always send their children to Hantsport's school. Their children were instead often sent by bus to school somewhere in the dark murky depths of Kings County. So, in a way, Halloween Eve was extra special because it was an occasion to meet our soul brothers – Brian, George, Michael, Tim, and others – from Hants Border.

At this point on Main Street, for most Halloweens, we would head out for Hants Border where several of the residents had mailboxes at the roadside. "Idea balloons" popped above our heads, like in the Bugs Bunny or Road Runner/Coyote cartoons on television and in the newspaper comics. We would place firecrackers inside the mailboxes, and blow them open. But inevitably, the balloon idea would prove to be a dud. The mailboxes were never blown open, but at best only served like an echo chamber to make the exploding firecracker sound louder.

However, on this particular Halloween, somebody from Main Street knew the location of a wagon, as in a "horse and wagon." There was a grocery store near the middle of Main Street, probably the smallest of the three grocery stores in Hantsport at that time, which depended upon a man to deliver groceries to customers by his horse and wagon. This Main Street kid pulled the wagon from its barn, and, with the help of others, began pulling it down the middle of Main Street towards the intersection with William Street. The rest of the gang tagged along behind.

With its large rubber tires, the wagon proved easy to pull and maneuver, and we turned down William Street. We picked up speed as we went. In the absence of traffic, with half-a-dozen kids pulling and another half-a-dozen pushing or just running along, we continued to pick up speed to the glee of all. We shouted out loud, "we are the kings of the road!" We had no sense of purpose, just enjoying ourselves by doing something that was totally different and unbelievable. We passed the Post Office on our right as we went down William Street, with the Oak Street intersection fast approaching. Our speed continued to pick up, faster and faster we went.

Oh, oh!

"Who are the clowns pulling this wagon?" somebody shouted, "They must be from the Main Street area of town, or Holmes Hill, or Hants Border, certainly not from this, the lower area of town."

After all, immediately ahead on William Street, just one building passed the Oak Street intersection, there was the fire-station with its door wide open and full of firefighters who were serving as temporary police officers. We were heading directly into the bowels of our own fire.

But as it turned out, the firefighters were probably overwhelmed by the suddenness of everything. The wagon and dozen-odd kids were moving as fast as humanly possible. Faster than a firefighter could complete his bite of a doughnut or finish his sip of coffee, we were gone like an alien UFO flashing through the sky. Onward we continued, over the William Street railroad crossing, we sped, maintaining our break-neck speed to the end of the street.

What, to the end of William Street? But William Street ended with a gravel road that went down a very steep hill to the government wharf and the Avon River. If the tide was out, there would be a major, death-like drop into the mud and gravel; and if the tide was in, we would be into frigidly cold, chocolate brown coloured and salty water. Did these clowns really know where we were heading? Fortunately, somebody up front had good enough sense to avoid the hill by turning sharply left at the last moment onto the gypsum company's parking lot that overlooked the river far below. We decided to leave the wagon in the parking lot, undamaged, where it could easily be found next day.

At about this time, the familiar sound went off – errrrhh-errrhh-errrhh – of the town's curfew siren. It was 10 PM, time for all good kids to be at home and off the street. I don't recall the curfew law ever being rigidly enforced; it was mainly a self-disciplinary mechanism for kids to remember to go home, especially on a school night. And on this night, we had had our fill of excitement, so we wandered home to enjoy our treats.

A RIVER RAN BY — "HANTSPORT-ON-THE-AVON"

"Hantsport-on-the-Avon," announced the conductor on the rail car as we entered the outskirts of Hantsport.

By 1970, the full service passenger train had long disappeared from usage. In its place, there was a so-called *Dayliner* operated by the Dominion Atlantic Railroad. With the decline of people using the train in the Annapolis Valley, the D. A. R. had started to use a single motorized carriage – sometimes two such carriages were connected to each other. I never knew the conductor's name, but he would announce the train's arrival in Hantsport with his unique call of "*Hantsport-on-the-Avon*." Of course, many passengers would make the immediate connection with Shakespeare's hometown of "Stratford-on-the-Avon," even though the "Avon" part is pronounced differently (*A' von* in England, and *Av' on* in Nova Scotia). Passengers enjoyed the conductor's folksy merry-making with quiet chuckles of recognition.

A boy's life in Hantsport during the 1950s and early 1960s was very much centred on the Avon River. It was, of course, nothing like earlier decades when there were ferries coming and going, shipyards building wooden ships that sailed the world, with nearby hotels for those in transit and numerous small businesses dependent upon seafaring. Oh, there were still some elderly citizens, like Miss Masters, who lived across the street from me, who could personally recall the town's earlier history of the late 19ᵗʰ and early 20ᵗʰ centuries. But awareness of such earlier history was completely foreign to my generation. By our time, the Avon was known mainly to us for its swimming beach, fishing and working wharves.

In addition, so as not to be confused, our Avon River was nothing like the narrow and gentile English river that flows through Stratford-on-the-Avon where you can easily see and talk with people on the opposite side. Neither was it anything like a Mark Twain narration of Tom Sawyer or Huckleberry Finn on the slow-moving Mississippi River as it meandered lazily through a pastoral countryside. No way! Our Avon River has always been known as being a rough-and-tumble river reportedly with the world's highest tides twice a day.

It is a river whose majesty must be respected, and not taken lightly! Yet the Avon River's diverse features allowed for multiple uses. The riverfront in the '50s and early '60s was thus a magnetic draw for boys in summertime, full with an endless array of attractions.

a. Beach

The sandy beach was a centre piece, or most public section, of the riverfront where, prior to the construction of the town's community swimming pool, we would take swimming lessons in the summer. The river water came directly from the Minas Basin, which is part of the Bay of Fundy. It even extended into the Atlantic Ocean and remained cold all summer long. How cold? It would probably have made Robert W. Service's "Sam McGee" character wish that he was back in the Yukon!

Oh, the sun tried – did it ever try – to warm the water, radiating streams of heat each summer day. But it was all of little avail. It took next to no time to get sunburn while taking swimming lessons. I once got sunburn on top of earlier sunburn from the previous day! Fortunately, however, doctors still made house calls at that time as I doubt if I could have gone from my sick bed to the doctor's office.

Though raw sewage was (and probably still is) dumped directly into the river, I don't remember anybody coming down with skin rashes. No doubt the sunburns were more immediate and were a greater priority for remedial attention, while sun rashes were overlooked.

In addition, and with the benefit of hindsight, I don't recall anybody contracting eye ailments from the polluted water, probably because we never swam under water with our eyes open. After all, the relentless ebb and flow of the tide continuously stirred the sand and mud. So the water was a constant milk-chocolate brown colour, with a strong salty taste, that made it absolutely impossible to see anything. Keep your eyes and mouth closed was a wise policy.

Nevertheless, as kids, we did develop a cautious respect for the magnitude of the Avon River's tides and its powerful under-currents. Once we became accustomed to the cold water, we never swam too far out – you could easily be swept out to deeper water. Besides, the swimming area was fortunately enclosed by a set of buoys strung together by a rope so that we would not stray out of bounds.

Given the river water's coldness, dangerous current, and sewage-related disease potential, the opening of the community swimming pool in 1955 came with great expectations. Actually, my father was employed to do the pipe-fitting and plumbing of the new facility. He thus had the opportunity to be the very first person to swim in the pool, although I don't believe he ever did so – at least not officially.

More inviting than the riverfront's swimming area, however, was the cliff that stood over the beach. Although there was a set of wooden steps for normal people to go up and down, six to eight year old boys are not "normal people". We would jump off the twenty-foot high cliff that had about a 70 degree slope to the beach below.

"Geronimo," Wray would shout as he took a flying leap into mid-air.

"Yeah", said Johnnie, "the sand on the side of the cliff is so soft, you just continue to slide until you reach the beach that is also so soft."

"And don't forget to shout 'Geronimo'", reminded Laurie, "that's what the soldiers shout in the movies when they parachute from airplanes."

Further down the beach westward toward the Minas Basin, there were rotten wood remnants of staging where ships had apparently been built back in the late 1800s and early 1900s during the town's heyday of ship building. At least, that was what we believed to be the origins of the remnants – it provided a romantic and mysterious, and most acceptable, explanation.

Meanwhile, although I don't recall seeing any fossils on the Hantsport beach, they have been found elsewhere on the banks of the Avon River – one of the best locations for fossils in all of eastern Canada is just a short distance away at Blue Beach. (Google "Blue Beach Fossil Museum.")

On the other side of the Hantsport beach, towards the gypsum company's fenced-in shed and wharf, there were rocks from which we would fish for smelts, Tommy cod, and eels. "But how do the fish know to stay here and not in the public swimming area where we take our swimming lessons?" asked Laurie.

"Yikes, that would be horrible to swim with the eels," interjected Johnnie.

"Don't be silly", offered Victor our fishing expert, "the buoys around the swimming area keep the eels and other fishes away and confined to the rocky shore."

"Are you serious?" questioned Laurie. "The fish swim in the water, deep below the buoys that are on top of the water."

"Well, the splashing of the swimmers scares the fish to the quieter water over here near the rocks," added Victor.

b. Wharves

The gypsum company's wharf and property were not easily accessible because of its fence. But it was great watching the gypsum ships arrive on the in-coming tide, maneuver to the wharf, receive a load of gypsum ore, and then depart on full tide.

There was, however, a second wharf – the government wharf – on the other side of the gypsum company's property, which was directly approachable through its main entrance on William Street. Actually, at the time, William Street simply ended to become a dirt road down a very steep hill, past the Minas Basin Pulp and Paper mill on the right, to the large concrete surfaced wharf on the riverfront.

This government wharf was probably our favourite riverfront attraction especially during the spring and summer months for different reasons. First, this wharf was, and still is, one of the best places to witness the magnitude of the largest tides in the world Ocean-going ships were still arriving regularly to pick up loads of pulp produced at the pulp mill, and we could get up close to watch everything. Since it would take a few days to load these pulp ships, there was a "bed" of rock and gravel upon which a ship rested for extra support when the tide went out. By the way, when the tide was out, it was possible albeit extremely muddy to walk around the hull of one of these ships.

The arrival of these pulp ships was always a fascinating time for other reasons. We met sailors from foreign lands and were introduced to previously unseen things, like chopsticks and soccer balls. Yes, as strange as it may now seem (in 2017), there were not many Chinese restaurants in the whole province of Nova Scotia during the '50s and early '60s, so few of us had experience with chopsticks. Likewise, neither was soccer a widely played game in the province; personally, I only played soccer for the first time in the fall of 1963, when I went to Windsor Regional High School for my last year of high school. Yet many visiting sailors would give out chopsticks and other gifts as a good-will gesture, and often playfully kick around a soccer ball, while waiting for the ship to be loaded.

Of equal interest, there was the fascination of watching the pulp ships being loaded. Dozens of men were hired to load a ship, each man maneuvering by hand a small cart to deliver one bale (probably weighing 700 - 800 lbs.) at a time from the pulp shed to the side of the ship. Then a large net would be used to hoist several bales at a time into the ship's hold.

We were much too young and small to get one of those jobs to wield a cart although the budding manhood inside us led us to think otherwise. Instead, we had to resign ourselves in summer to mixing jugs of "Kool-Aid" to sell to the thirsty workers at five cents a glass (with no free refills). Just the same, it was necessary to be cautious at this job location.

On one occasion when I was not present, a classmate, John, slipped from the wharf when the tide was out and fell onto the deck of a ship, breaking his back. Fortunately, he fully recovered and became a top-notch pitcher able to throw curve balls on our baseball teams – we would joke good-naturally about how his pitching performance was connected to his break.

Besides watching the loading of pulp ships, fishing from the government wharf was always good when the tide was in. Or if the tide was out, we would climb down one of the wharf's steel ladders to the muddy river bed. Smelts were our favourite catch as they were much tastier than Tommy cod. In fact, we sometimes would cut up a freshly caught Tommy cod on the spot to be used as bait as an alternative to worms.

Once, while fishing from the muddy river bed, I had unbelievable luck bringing in a smelt with each and every cast. No exaggeration, each and every cast brought in a smelt. Little did I know at the time that I was standing on an old wooden sewage outlet and, with each cast, my baited hook and line was landing in the spot where the fish were feeding on the raw sewage.

Meanwhile on that same occasion, Laurie who was fishing near by was having absolutely no luck at all. No luck, that is, until Drew or Bill baited his hook for him; the twins looked so much alike that now I can't remember which one baited the hook. In any case, with the very next cast, Laurie caught a smelt with the hook through the tip of the fish's tail – quite a first catch!

In the summer when the tide was in, the tugboat, *Otis Whack*, was often tied up to the government wharf. Older boys like "Popsi" and "Spike" demonstrated their bravery by climbing as high as possible onto the cabin roof of the *Otis Whack*. These were their actual nick-names, by the way; in fact, Spike's younger and shorter brother was called "Tack."

In any case, from the top of the *Otis Whack*, "Popsi" and "Spike" would dive off or jump as a "cannonball" into the water below, shouting the now familiar refrain "Geronimo" with each effort. As smaller and younger boys, our gang could only stare with open-mouthed amazement, especially when on occasion a head-first dive was accomplished rather than a butt-first cannonball.

No doubt this ability to climb high on a boat and to dive off provided Popsi with all the job training required when he was hired a couple of years later as a crew member of the replica of the *Bounty*. He sailed off for Tahiti for the filming of Marlon Brando's 1962 movie version of *Mutiny on the Bounty*. Popsi later returned as a local celebrity appearing at local movie theatres for showings of the newly released movie.

c. The Funny-Book Shed

While playing on the beach, fishing, and diving were seasonal events and the arrival of gypsum and pulp ships was occasional, the main riverfront attraction was the Funny-Book Shed. Compared to other pulp and paper plants, the production capacity of the Minas Basin Pulp and Power plant was relatively small. But it did have the capacity to recycle used paper – long before recycling became a popular activity in the early 21st century. Tons of used paper in large bales of 500 to 700 lbs. or more would be collected from all over Nova Scotia and deposited in a special shed that we called the Funny-Book Shed waiting to be recycled.

These bales would be stacked about five high by fork-lift trucks in a large shed. As kids, we had about half-a-dozen ways to sneak into this storage facility. There was a side door that usually remained open during the day that we sometimes used. A couple of other ways that we used were from the main production floor above the shed. When nobody was looking, we would slip down a spiral staircase into the Funny-Book Shed below. Or sometimes, if it wasn't in use, we would simply walk down a conveyor belt. But the easiest and most accessible entry point was right through the main door of the shed. This door was always wide open during the day, and the workers inside were usually pre-occupied working in the interior of the building rather than being at the door.

Then, once inside, we would climb to the top of the bales, high up near the ceiling and out of sight. Why? What's the point of it all? And why was it called the "Funny-Book Shed"?

Well, these questions are fair and deserve to be answered. So let's jump back a couple of paragraphs to my mention of the tons of used paper collected from across the province and brought in large bales to be recycled.

The used paper included newspapers, magazines, and comic books which retailers had not been able to sell. That's right, comic books, or "funny-books" as we called them, were mixed inside many of the bales of used paper. The funny-books were thus free for the taking. Well, they were sort of free, or at least they were available for the taking, in our way of thinking. The only trick was not to be caught, and so we had the different routes through which to sneak into the building. Then, once on top of the bales and out of sight, we would dig inside the bales until we found a treasure trove of funny-books.

These funny-books were in very good condition except that their front covers had been removed. Apparently, a retailer would remove the front covers of unsold comics to be returned to the publisher to claim some kind of reimbursement. The retailer would then trash the remainder of the funny-books through the recycling process. Whatever the case, we certainly were not bothered by the missing front covers.

It was an afternoon of pure delight digging into each bale trying to find the one bale with the largest bonanza. Often a bale would be a dud containing only newspapers, newsmagazines, or crossword puzzle magazines, which we would often take home for our parents with no questions asked. As well, in our early, pre-puberty years, we were most disappointed with adult magazines of partially naked women. Though in later years, older boys would explain things to us – sex education in Hantsport-on-the-Avon, '50s and '60s style!

But our prime targets were the funny-books, whether our favourites were cowboys, animal cartoon characters, or super-action figures. Even the "classic comic," where a famous novel was shortened and transcribed to comic-book format, was to be found on occasion. They were all there for the taking.

I don't think any boy ever purchased comics in Hantsport; there was no need to do so. With each visit to the Funny-Book Shed, each of us would find twenty, thirty, or more comics of interest. We would stuff them inside our shirts or jackets to be hidden from view just in case we should meet plant workers. Then when the exit was clear, we would scoot out of the shed and nonchalantly walk home. The supply of comics would last for several weeks, until we had another urge to visit our unique comic book store.

Such then was a kid's life centred on the riverfront in Hantsport-on-the-Avon in the 1950s and early 1960s. It was a rite of passage that has since disappeared. The construction of the outdoor swimming pool ended swimming lessons on the beach; very few people explore or wander along the riverfront area. Neither the pulp ships nor gypsum ships come and dock anymore. The fish are left largely untouched, free to swim in the polluted, murky brown water of the mighty Avon River. And kids no longer have the opportunity to fathom the delights of the Funny-Book Shed.

8

TREK TO INDIAN GRAVEYARD

I don't know why it was called "Indian Graveyard" but there it was down along the railroad track on the eastern edge of town. It was a small piece of wooded land, not much greater than a baseball outfield in size. The site was cut off from the mainland by the railroad track. It was like – albeit not actually – a little, squared island with mud-flats and marsh grass on three sides which were often flooded when the tide was in especially during the spring of a year. The railroad track was along the remaining side.

During the 1950s and early 1960s, this railroad was still heavily used by passenger and mail trains, freight trains and ore trains carrying gypsum rock. The Dominion Atlantic Railroad track ran right through Hantsport extending from the major provincial city of Halifax on the Atlantic Ocean at one end and down through the Annapolis Valley to Digby and Yarmouth at the other end. Shipping connections to the rest of the world were at both ends of this railroad. The ebb and flow of life in Hantsport (and the other valley towns) had for decades been centred on these steel rails and trains.

Those of us from the lower, industrial part of the town, between the Avon River and the tracks, were quite familiar with this dependency on the rails. We saw and heard the trains several times each day, and we often had to wait at the railroad crossings as freight and ore trains shunted back and forth as individual cars were either connected or disconnected.

Often we would be delayed getting to school, waiting for the engineers and train workers to give us opportunity to cross the tracks. How slow were those shunting trains especially at the William Street crossing? When nobody was looking, we would break the monotony of waiting by placing a penny on a rail track to be flattened by the train. Of course, given the slow movement of those heavy, shunting behemoths, there was no danger that a small penny would tip over a train. But I will leave it to each reader to imagine what the penny looked like after being squashed by a train. Then there was the occasion when the daring and adventurous Geoff claimed to have hopped onto the ladder outside the end of one slow-moving freight car, and hanged on for a free trip to Windsor about seven miles away.

Accustomed as we were to the frequent trains crossing Prince and William streets, it was so inviting for kids to take a summer trek down the railroad tracks to that mysterious clump of woods called Indian Graveyard. Not that we ever expected to find actual graves of Indians (or anybody else), we did often wonder speculatively about some curious indentations in the earth at that site. Were these depressions former graves, or were they spots dug by people looking for First Nation arrow heads? The imaginations of young boys had no limitations!

I suppose that the site's "island-like" appearance was what caught our attention the most. A self-contained location on the horizon that could easily be seen from the town was a place we just had to explore. As is often the case, the joy of trekking to Indian Graveyard was mainly in the actual trek itself, and not so much as in actually being there. It was like a rainbow where the real attraction is in beholding the beauty of the spectrum of colours, not with finding an actual pot of gold.

A straight, no-nonsense walk down the tracks from the railroad crossing at Prince Street to Indian Graveyard would probably take fifteen minutes. I say "probably" because I don't know for certain. You see, as kids, we never took a straight, no-nonsense trek. Instead, our trek to Indian Graveyard would actually take all afternoon. It was an escape from the regularity or tameness of town life, and a chance to be out on our own. It fed our taste for youthful adventure.

Usually, everything would begin on a hot, humid summer afternoon in August, when somebody would whine, "I am bored, there is nothing to do." To which, another would respond, "let's go to Indian Graveyard." There was little if any discussion, and certainly no debate, of the suggestion but only shared agreement.

Laurie would say, "We must take along a gun and ammunition in order to take pot shots on the way." Wray would add, "Does anybody have a pellet or BB rifle, or what about a .22 rifle?" Somebody would inevitably have a rifle plus extra ammo.

So as we left my home walking toward the railroad crossing on Prince Street, we physically closed ranks, walking shoulder to shoulder, with the gun owner in the centre holding the rifle vertically pointed down to the ground next to the side of his left leg. That way, the town clerk (Mr. Eric Smith) and the police chief (Mr. Allard) in the town hall on our right would not notice the gun. Of course, having learned the proper use of firearms since the age of eight or ten, we walked with the rifle's ammunition chamber empty and with the safety lock in place Once we got to the Prince Street crossing, we were home-free with no further houses or adults to worry about, only Indian Graveyard on the horizon at the end of our trek beckoned us.

Within a minute or two, there was a patch of blackberry bushes on our right. We had to stop to feast before going any further; no need to undertake a journey on an empty stomach.

"Oh good, the blackberries are ripe, and look at the size of them."

"Yeah, it only takes three or four of these "doozers" to fill the hand!"

"Ah, I don't like them – their big black bumps remind me of those big, black ants."

"Don't be silly, just taste their sweetness."

"If you see ants, just brush them off."

Next on our trek, there were the garbage dumps. First, there was a mainly industrial dump on the left, on a small inlet of the Avon River. It often proved to be a wonderful place to scrounge around in, for a half hour or so. Finding unusual objects always proved without fail the old adage of "one person's trash is another person's treasure!"

"But what if we see a rat?"

"Well, we have the rifle, don't we?"

"So you had better load the gun now."

"But we can't stay long at this dump. We must quickly get a move on."

Then a short distance further along, on the right side of the tracks, there was the dumpsite of some town residents who lived on top of a cliff on Porter's Avenue and who threw their garbage over and down the cliff side. "Out of the way, out of sight" was the only rule for garbage removal in those days, though I always suspected that it was a lousy greeting to the town for train passengers to see. We usually ignored this second dump because it was a bit further away from the railroad tracks. And if Victor was with us, he saw no excitement in routing through the garbage that he had just tossed over the cliff earlier in the day. Besides, there was a more inviting target between the tracks and the residential dump – a pond!

Is it possible for kids to ignore a pond? I don't think so. "Last spring, this pond was full of minnows, tadpoles, and pollywogs," said Johnnie.

"I know," I said, "Laurie and I took many of them home as pets."

"Yeah," said Laurie, "but the minnows all died, and the tadpoles or pollywogs turned into miniature toads that hopped away."

"Hey, look over here," shouted Wray, "look at this hole in the mud bank. It must be the hole to the home of muskrats."

To which, Bobby inquired, "can you look into the hole to see a muskrat; I have never seen a muskrat."

"Don't be silly;" replied Wray, "it is too dark in the hole to see very far."

"Yeah," added Victor, who seemed to know the most about wildlife, "muskrat homes are deep, deep down, and not near the outdoor entrance. Also, muskrats build several entrance holes to their homes so that, if people or foxes are at one entrance, they always have other escape routes."

Regardless of the discussion, we seldom if ever saw muskrats in the light of day, and, if necessary, we had our trusty gun, not to mention sticks and stones to defend ourselves. So, with the absence of wildlife on this occasion, we left the pond and resumed our trek, with few additional diversions. Still, we made it a most enjoyable walk.

Sometimes we would balance ourselves by walking along one steel rail. Other times, we would step on each and every wooden tie and, then alternatively, with giant steps on every second tie. Or possibly, from time to time, we would put our ear on the rail to hear if a train was coming, just like we had seen in the western movies on Saturday afternoons at the theatre. To our left, there were the mud-flats of the mighty Avon River or brown coloured water if the tide was in, and, to our right, the marsh land on both sides of the narrow Halfway River.

According to kid lore, the Halfway River was called halfway because it was half way between where you are now and an equal distance away on the over side of the river. Such was the remarkable logic of young children – simple, direct, and it made sense, with a laugh at the end. You had to be an eight or ten-year old to appreciate the joke. Besides, the Halfway River was actually the halfway point of our trek. (Interestingly, the "truth" of the matter is not much different – the Halfway River was so named because it was about halfway between the larger settlements of Windsor and Grand Pré back in the 1700s and 1800s.)

In any case, at the juncture of the Avon and Halfway rivers, the railroad tracks crossed the Halfway River by going over a very small wooden railroad bridge which was known locally as the aboideau (or aboideaux). Once we arrived at this aboideau, we stopped our trek, eagerly looking both ways for the appearance of a train. Yes, we wanted a train to appear at this very moment in our afternoon outing. That is why earlier we had placed our ears to the rail track in hopes of hearing an approaching train. We were not simply aping what we had seen in those western movies, but we were applying the lessons learned and hoping for a train to come along.

If a train appeared at this point, we would scurry over the side of the tracks and down the side of the bridge for one of our greatest adventures that a kid could imagine. We would climb onto a small wooden ledge on top of the aboideau, and stretch out. That way, with the train rumbling less than one yard or metre above us, whistle blowing, with the ground trembling and white steam enshrouding us, we felt so brave and manly while being "run over." Thankfully, however, nobody in a passenger train ever flushed the toilet at that moment in time. (The flushed droppings at that time left the train and fell outside the train onto the rail bed.)

With that little adventure over, our trek started again. To our right was the marsh land that was often flooded in the spring by the Halfway River. To our left, there were vast mud-flats of the Avon River which were especially spacious when the tide was out. The Avon River, connected as it is to the Minas Basin that in turn is part of the Bay of Fundy, has reportedly the highest tides in the world. The communities on both sides of the Avon had been the birthplace of countless wooden ships in the age of "wind and sail." In fact, modern ocean-going ships were still regularly arriving at Hantsport during our time. Twice a day, the tide came in and went out, ceaselessly stirring the silt, giving the river water a constant chocolate brown colour. Left fully exposed when the tide was out, the mud-flats extended as far as the eye could see.

At other times and locations, we would take off our socks and sneakers, to run and slide on this mud or just to stand still. We liked to feel the mud ooze between the toes while sinking ankle deep or deeper. But such was not the case today with our trek to Indian Graveyard. Instead, this was an occasion to sit on the railroad bed and use the rifle. Whether it was a BB gun, a pellet gun, or a .22 repeater rifle, we were now far enough away from town to target practice. Bottles, driftwood, and other debris left behind by the last tide and now stuck in the mud-flats served as targets, or, if the tide was in, floating debris would serve instead as targets. Sharing the rifle, Laurie, Johnnie, Wray, Bill, Bobby, Darrell, Victor, my brother Graham, and I would take pot shots at the targets.

We each took turns cocking and loading the gun, aiming and then squeezing the trigger. Since it was my gun on this occasion, I had the first go:

Click, click …. Puff …. then … SPLAT!

Then the others would have their opportunity in turn to shoot:

Click, click …. Puff …. SPLAT!

Click, click …. Puff …. SPLAT!

We all knew how to handle the gun – the clicking sound of cocking the bullet into the gun chamber, and the sound of the bullet being released as we squeezed (not pulled) the trigger. More often than not since we usually missed the target, the bullet would land with a big splat in the mud or water. The splat sound was preceded by the sight of mud or water splashing in all directions. Hey, our school teacher actually did know what she was talking about: sight does travel faster than sound.

"I almost hit the target; I'll do better next time."

"I came closer than you did."

"I never miss; so the sight must be off and needs adjusting."

"Let me try. I am a great shooter because I shot half-a-dozen rabbits last winter."

"Oh, you only got those rabbits because you used a shotgun that sprayed pellets, not a single bullet."

"Did not."

"Did so."

"I am still a better shooter than you."

The pot-shooting competition was simply a fun activity with a bit of competition thrown in. To look at a target some distance away, to line up the rifle sights, to steady one's arms and regulate one's breathing, and then to squeeze the trigger. Did we hit the target? And if not, then how close did we come?

When we ran out of ammo, we continued the last bit of the trek to Indian Graveyard. But there was still one last side trip. Directly opposite Indian Graveyard on the right side of the steel rails, we scampered up the hill side of Mt. Denson. Here, there was another blackberry patch that grew the largest, most luscious blackberries in the world! And on top of the hill, there was a mature apple orchard at its prime, producing apples so large that one apple would fill both hands.

With our second feast over, we went back down the hill, crossed the tracks, and finally entered Indian Graveyard. Once there, we ran unchecked encircling the outskirts of the territory, uttering sounds of triumph. Then we wandered through the inland woods. Each of us found a tree and, as privately as possible, had a piss. As only boys can, we marked our possession. We did not know the origins of the phrase, "possession is nine-tenths the law," but the words suddenly had significance to us. Once again, we ran back and forth across the island, only now it was "our" island!

We wished once again that we had brought a shovel to dig into those strange indentations. Who knows, we might have uncovered Indian arrowheads or other hidden wonders possibly pirate treasure. But nobody really cared if we found any such treasures. The afternoon was almost over. It was time to head home as supper time was soon approaching. Being at Indian Graveyard was anti-climatic; our delight had been as always wrapped with the trek, with every step of that trek.

Our return journey home was usually uneventful except for again balancing on the rails or stepping on the rail ties. If lucky, another train would come along at the right time for us to be "run over" again at the Aboideaux Bridge. Our thirst for freedom and adventure had been quenched by the trek to Indian Graveyard.

9

OUR FURRY, SLIMY, AND FEATHERY COMPANIONS

Humans and animals have lived together around the world throughout the ages. As James Herriot related in his charming stories about a British veterinarian, which became the basis for a long-running television series, animals come in many different forms both great and small in size. Being a small rural town in Nova Scotia during the 1950s and early 1960s, it is not surprising that Hantsport residents were well acquainted with animals.

We learned to distinguish at an early age between domestic and wild animals, as well as between animals that were pets, pests, or sources of food. Many of the older houses in Hantsport at that time still had a barn where horse, wagon, and hay had been kept in earlier days. Our neighbour, Mr. Johnston, still raised chickens for egg production on a small scale in a coop behind his house. We were used to real animals, and not taken in with fictional portraits like Walt Disney's *Bambi*.

Dogs and cats still ran loose and few had identity tags. Such tags were not required because everybody knew their names and their respective homes and owners. A few individuals even kept a horse as a pet; though my first pet was a rabbit. Others kept gold fish, turtles, white rats, hamsters and budgies as pets. Sometimes, we caught wildlife like tadpoles, minnows and pigeons that we would then raise as pets.

Everybody seemed to possess at least one animal as a pet. But at the same time, we realized that other animals were for eating. We went fishing all through the summertime, and sometimes rabbit hunting in the winter. Parents and others went deer, pheasant and partridge hunting every fall. Yet other animals were pests that had to be eliminated. We set mouse traps for mice that invariably came inside houses for warmth when the weather turned colder in the late fall.

All in all, however, some of our more interesting animal experiences were of the off-beat kind, not the daily routine kind.

a. "How much is that doggie in the window?"

Taste in popular music during the '50s and '60s may best be described as being eclectic. All sorts of music genre were listen to and enjoyed. This was evident as we had our Sunday noontime dinner every week while listening to a radio station that played each week's top ten music hits. Popular songs could have a country or folk flavour, or be of an instrumental or religious nature. Crooning songs as well as doo-wop and early rock-and-roll were also heard on the hit charts. Then there was the so-called British music invasion and anti-war protest songs of the '60s which were also equally appreciated.

Patti Page's rendition in 1952 of "How much is that doggie in the window?" was one of my family's all-time favourites. Was it the simplicity of the song's lyrics that made it so appealing? Or was it the clarity of Page's presentation? Or possibly it was the connection that the public had with dogs, especially when we heard the dog's cute "arf, arf" barking sound inserted as Page sang the song's lyrics.

I must quickly add, however, that the idea of a pet store was absolutely foreign to us. There was no pet store in Hantsport; we had never seen or heard of a pet store elsewhere. The case of chicks being sold in hardware store windows was a rarity (see below), although it did occur two or three successive Easters in Hantsport and in other locations. These hardware store chick sales were the closest we ever had to a pet store.

My family was primarily a "cat family" usually possessing at least one or two cats at a time. When a cat had kittens, kids had the responsibility to go knocking on doors to give the kittens away. This was how people acquired most pets, through "giveaways" from friends and neighbours, not at pet stores.

However, we did have an assortment of other pets over the years, including three dogs, a rabbit and turtles. My brother Graham and his friends used to capture and raise pigeons in our barn. Also, for a time, my sister Pam provided "daycare" for dogs and horses when their owners went away during the summer. In addition, since I had aspired for many years to become a veterinarian, I had some farm experience working with cattle, sheep, and pigs.

b. Tadpoles in a Pink Baby Bath Tub

For many years, as an annual habit, we would capture minnows at a pond near the Halfway River just a short distance from the railroad tracks. Our intention was to raise the minnows like an inexpensive version of goldfish. But we never had any success. Within two or three weeks, the minnows would be floating belly up, dead. So one spring, instead of minnows, we decided to catch some tadpoles (or pollywogs, as they are sometimes called). We had much greater success with their survival rate. Well, actually, we did lose them but they didn't all die due to their captivity with us.

Every year, during the last few days of winter or the first days of spring, when you never knew what season it was, something special would happen. The Halfway River would flood its banks. Nobody really cared because there was not much to worry about. People did not have homes on that river's banks; and the marsh land was only used later in the summer for haying. So the annual flooding was only to be watched in wonderment, with nothing to be worried about.

But the annual flood was a signal to kids. Once the flood had receded, a pond would be left behind. It would be our opportunity to capture minnows and tadpoles, or we could just teasingly chase the little critters around the pond. I wouldn't say that chasing them was cruel or mean. After all, being chased around by a bunch of noisy kids must have been more entertaining for the tadpoles and minnows than being eaten by muskrats and other animals. If anything, the chase only strengthened their swimming muscles and skills to escape their potential real killers.

In any case, on this one particular occasion, we decided to catch tadpoles and to raise them at home as pets. Technically, in biological terms, tadpoles are the larvae of amphibians such as frogs and toads. In size, depending on the number of days since evolving from their egg stage, tadpoles were smaller than the circumference of a finger nail. They were bulbous in shape, with a head and body indistinguishable with everything together in just one round bulb. Everything, that is except for a long tail that was about the same length as the bulb part of the tadpole. Given its solid black colour and shiny appearance, a tadpole usually looked like a miniature whale as you see in cartoons, but not in real life.

To see these little shiny black and cute-looking creatures dart through the pond water made them prime targets. We just had – as in "must" – to take these animals home with us to be our pets. After all, in the wild, these critters had no protective parents looking after them. So we found an empty jar, and scooped up some tadpoles and pond water. Once home, we had to decide on a more permanent arrangement. The jar was obviously too small, and we did not have a proper aquarium.

My mother gave us permission to use an old pink baby bath tub that had been used when my sister was a baby. So we went back to the pond for more tadpoles and pond water. We also used a garden hose to fill the bath tub with additional water. Then we added some stones that partially projected above the water surface, in order to be like the wild pond. We also purchased some fish food from a hardware store, and daily we sprinkled the food into the tub. Our intention was good but I don't know if the tadpoles ever ate the fish food. Then the real fun began for the next few weeks.

Unlike reading a book on the biological evolution of amphibians or taking a biology course at school, we observed in real time the actual maturing of these tadpoles. Bit by bit each day, we noticed that their tails got shorter and thicker. Then two little appendices began to appear at the base of the bulbous body near the tail, and two other appendices began to appear near the front of the bulbous body. Gradually, the tail of each tadpole disappeared completely while the four appendices became legs. The shiny black bulb of the body was also replaced by a definite frog or toad form. Our tadpoles had turned into small, miniature frogs or toads before our very eyes; and each was about one inch square in size. I am afraid that we never learned whether these creatures were frogs or toads; though I suspect they were the latter as they liked living out of the water.

These miniature toads then started to hop up and over the sides of the pink baby bath tub, as they attempted to escape naturally into the wilds. Of course, being located in town, there was no wild place into which to escape and no pond. The little critters were going by natural instinct, not a map of the town. We did our best to put them back into the tub; also, we placed additional rocks in the tub to serve invitingly as rest locations.

Graham: "Oh, look at that, they are all around the tub this morning. They must have jumped out last night."

Laurie: "Quick, put them back. Or the cats and birds will get them."

Victor: "Yeah, I saw some crows and seagulls nearby when I came over this morning."

Laurie: "Hey, did you see that? One toad just jumped up. And I caught it in mid-air."

Stewart: "I never knew that toads could fly!"

Graham: "Oh, oh. Over there is a dead toad. I wonder if a cat killed it, and left the body instead of eating it."

Victor: "Well, we can get a shovel and bury that dead toad and others in our pet graveyard behind the barn."

But we could not be present 24 hours a day, so a countless number of those creatures did escape. I suspect also that birds and cats preyed on these tasty morsels of food. Eventually, we took the surviving critters back to the pond and released them close to their brothers and sisters near their original home.

c. Up the Creek in Smelts

Fishing was always a big part of our life on the Avon River during the summertime months. We fished primarily for smelts, although we would often catch Tommy cods and eels. I don't know if "Tommy cod" was simply a local name but it was a small fish with little resemblance to the much bigger cod caught by the major commercial fishing industry. As well, sometimes my father took the family to the upper reaches of the Halfway River in Bishopville for freshwater fishing of trout or to dams for fishing of bass. At that time, there was no requirement to purchase and possess a fishing license, so you went fishing whenever the mood struck.

If we didn't have a rod and reel, we would cut a long pole and tie a fishing line to the pole with a hook and worm as bait. Sometimes we connected a red and white plastic bobber to detect when a fish was nibbling or when a fish had been hooked. But a bobber was not always necessary. Simply holding part of the line loosely in your spare hand served the same purpose of detecting a fish on the line. Actually, it was tantalizing to hold the line in your hand because you could feel the initial gentle nibbling of the fish as it tasted the bait and then the sudden yank when it was hooked.

On one occasion, we were fishing from an old scow tied to a little-used wharf on the Avon River. I didn't have a proper rod and reel, and there was no near-by thin tree or branch to cut for a fishing pole. So I simply tied an end of a fishing line to my right index finger, and dangled the other end with hook and bait in the water by holding my arm over the edge of the scow. It worked! I still have to this day an old family movie of me dancing up and down in excitement atop the scow after hauling in a fish.

Besides catching fish one at a time, our father would take us annually in the springtime to the Gaspereau River to scoop dozens of smelts with each scoop. Located about half-way between Hantsport and the town of Wolfville, the Gaspereau River was narrow in size and its banks were easily accessible. Each year, tens of thousands of smelts and other fish species like gaspereau (sometimes called alewife) would come from the ocean up the rivers off the Bay of Fundy to spawn. The Gaspereau River was an ideal spot to dip for these fish. By using a home-made dip net, consisting of a long-handled pole and a firmly attached basket made out of chicken-wire, a strong and skilful person like my father was able to scoop dozens of smelts at a time. The dip net, however, was usually too heavy and awkward for my brother Graham and me. So we were lucky to catch one or two smelts with each attempt, yet it was still an exciting time.

Once, while driving along the road, my father noticed an accessible spot close to the Gaspereau River. After parking to approach the river bank, my father then remarked: "Look at that small island in the middle of the river. The island's edge is closer to the edge of the river. So it would be easier to scoop the smelts over there."

Graham noted: "Also, the river isn't deep across to the island."

Stewart: "Yes, you can even see schools of smelts go by. Look at them; there must be thousands in each school."

Father: "With your calf-high rubber boots, you two will be able to wade over to the island with no difficulty. With my hip-high boots, I am okay. So I will take the dip net and the containers."

We were having great success. My father was scooping dozens of smelts with each dip. Graham and I were equally busy picking-up and placing the smelts into the containers. We were oblivious, however, to what was going on around us. Finally, I took notice of the situation: "Oh, oh, isn't the island getting smaller?"

Graham: "Yeah, look at the island shoreline. It is getting smaller by the second, and the river water is getting deeper."

Father: "Somebody upriver must have opened the dam. We had better get off the island and back to the main riverbank."

Stewart: "But the river water is now too deep for my boots."

Graham: "It is also too deep for my boots"

Father: "I am okay with my hip rubber boots. So I will carry you two to the roadside of the river. Then I will come back for the dip net and the containers of smelts."

We had been up the creek in trouble. By the time we were safely on the roadside of the river, our once solid island had completely disappeared. No doubt, new schools of smelts were already swimming over where we had once stood. Or possibly the smelts had even stopped to deposit their eggs in the stony former island.

d. Why Build a Better Mouse Trap?

I grew up mainly in a spacious, older house that had been built in the late 1800s reputedly by a sea captain. As kids, we were always poking around, and would often make fascinating discoveries in hidden nooks and crannies, abandoned root cellars, and closed-off attics. One of our most treasured discoveries was an old, dirty, colour-faded mouse trap.

We were well accustomed with the standard modern mouse trap that consisted of a rectangular piece of flat wood, metal spring, bait holder, and killer loop that snaps over the mouse. The design of our discovered old-fashioned mouse trap, however, was marvelous. It was designed like a guillotine, and was capable of catching four mice at one setting!

The wood portion of this old-fashioned trap was round in shape, approximately five to six inches in diameter. It was also about one inch thick and mainly hollowed-out underneath. The most distinctive feature was the presence of four holes drilled in a north-south-west-east alignment on the rounded side of the trap. At each hole, there was a metal spring and loop, along with a trip wire to hold the loop in position. Bait was attached to the other end of the trip wire.

When a mouse smelled the bait, it would stick its head through the hole to grab the bait. This would release the trip wire and the spring would snap up the loop instantly and lethally around the mouse's neck or chest. Although this trap could hypothetically guillotine a mouse at each of the four holes, no doubt the first snap would most likely scare other mice away. Just the same, my personal record was three mice in one evening.

The effectiveness of this four-header mouse trap over the years had a major impact on the mouse problem. Every fall, mice would leave the fields and barn for the greater warmth to be found in the house. Our cats were more pets than great mousers, so we had to use mouse traps.

Otherwise, the mice would gnaw the wood and electrical wiring, and get into our food supply.

e. "Son, I say son, 'I ain't a chicken, I'm a rooster!'"

I do not recall the year when it was first released, but there was a *Foghorn Leghorn* cartoon in which the main rooster character encountered a young chicken hawk. This chicken hawk was pesky, determined to earn its wings as a true chicken hawk by catching its first chicken. According to the chicken hawk's picture book directions, Foghorn Leghorn certainly looked like a chicken. So the little chicken hawk tried every trick there was to make its first catch. If only the chicken hawk had taken a sex education course on gender identification, he would have saved himself a lot of trouble.

In any case, there was an occasion in the mid-1950s, at Easter time, that the town's two hardware stores started to sell chicks. These chicks were newly hatched and still without feathers. They were instead covered by fluff that had been dyed different colours. Each chick was coloured red, pink, blue, green, yellow, or purple. Can you spell "CUTE" in capital letters with an exclamation point at the end, while saying "Ah"?

Placed in a pen with a heat lamp, these chicks were on full display in each hardware store's front window for all passersby to see. Children were obviously the main audience target. My parents purchased three, one for each child (as my youngest sibling had yet to be born). We got to choose the chick of our favourite colour.

The hardware stores also sold packages of food for customers to feed the chicks, and chicken wire for cages. As keepers of the chicks, we were very successful as the three chicks thrived. Even as they lost their cuteness as the coloured fluff was replaced by white feathers, we conscientiously took care of the young birds. Some friends were less successful as some of their chicks died. Other friends grew bored with the chicks especially after they had molted their fluff, and gave their birds to us. By summertime, we had about a dozen birds.

Quite frankly, however, these birds were a tiresome bore to be with. None had a distinct personality. Neither could you play with them like a dog or cat. There was no eye connection or recognition with the fowl.

We built space in the barn to house the birds with an extension to a chicken-wired outdoor pen. At other times, we actually shepherded them around the house and barn allowing our "dirty dozen" to scratch fresh ground in search of slugs, other bugs and seeds, as they would naturally do if outdoors on their own. All summer long this went on. But our birds never laid an egg nor did they ever show an inclination to do so.

To echo Foghorn Leghorn, all twelve members of our flock were roosters, not chicken or laying hens!

10

THE TOWN OF INDUSTRIES ..... UH, MAKE THAT, "THEME PARK PLAYGROUNDS"

"**H**antsport – the Town of Industries" was the wording on the highway sign that greeted visitors or those simply driving through during the 1950s and early '60s. The sign was also a source of pride for locals returning home – a reminder of who we were. Hantsporters were a hard-working and enterprising people with a distinguished past, and numerous successful current industries and businesses to show for their efforts.

Unfortunately, in recent years, the earlier road sign has been replaced by another, "Haven of Hospitality." No doubt, this wording was penned by a graduate of a greeting card academy. The wording is hardly a distinguishing statement that sets Hantsport apart. The brand logo could have been applied just as easily to any other community that had lost its sense of direction and was waiting to re-invent itself.

For children in the 1950s and early 1960s, however, Hantsport's industrial sites also served as our playgrounds. It was like having a different amusement theme park for each day of the week. Gypsum, apples, lumber, and paper were the main playgrounds.

Just the same, some industrial operations were clearly "no go" zones. They were either largely inaccessible or had no appealing "play" features for kids. Yet other operations were so down-right dangerous, we had enough common sense to stay away.

a. Gypsum

My family lived for most of our time in Hantsport on William Street, between the riverfront and the main railroad tracks. The slow moving trains would often block both vehicle and pedestrian traffic. It was especially bad when a freight or gypsum ore train would shunt back and forth, adding or taking off cars onto side holding tracks in the rail yard. So we were often delayed going to school or church, to the Post Office or movie theatre, or to go shopping.

It was often tempting to crawl under a stopped or slow-moving rail car so as not to be late. But we weren't that crazy! We instead waited patiently a few steps back safely out of the way. Eventually the train workers would take pity on us by moving the train far enough back or ahead for us to pass.

Sometimes, however, we would break our boredom while waiting with some entertainment. We would place a penny or nail on a rail. What would happen when the monstrous and heavy train rolled over the small metal object? Would the penny be completely flattened or squashed with its inscriptions wiped off? Would the nail be cut in two? Just what would happen? Other times, we would place a hand-sized chunk of gypsum rock on a rail and watched it being pulverized into chalk-like dust.

The gypsum rail cars brought tons of ore from the gypsum mines, and would then be placed on a side holding rail tracks. Eventually, the ore rail cars would be taken onto the gypsum company's property for unloading. The cars would be unloaded in a small shed where the gypsum would be dumped down a chute; then an enclosed conveyor belt would take the ore into a gigantic storage shed that still can be seen from kilometers away. Bulldozers inside this storage shed would then spread out the mini-mountains of gypsum ore to maximize the use of available space. Later, other conveyor belts took the ore to be loaded into the holds of gypsum ships to be transported to processing facilities located primarily in the United States. Since only a wire fence separated the gypsum company property from my family's property, we watched as children the unloading of the rail cars so often that we could have done it ourselves while blind-folded. Meanwhile, although the unloading operation was "normal" with us, such was not the case with overnight visitors.

Like any host, my mother would inevitably say good morning to an overnight guest, asking "how well did you sleep, last night?"

To which the overnight guest would reply, "I didn't sleep a wink. What was that noise all night long?"

Mother: "Noise? What noise? Oh, do you mean the gypsum train being unloaded? We are so used to that, we never hear it. We sleep right through the unloading activity." Sure enough, by the second or third night of their stay, our guests would have become sufficiently accustomed to the noise to have a peaceful sleep.

The whole gypsum operation in Hantsport was fascinating to observe. But because it was so heavily mechanized, we kept a safe distance away and simply observed everything. Actually, we could easily watch the unloading of rail cars from our side of the fence, and there were absolutely no play opportunities to be had in the unloading shed. Neither was there anything for us in the large storage shed, just gigantic mounds of gypsum ore waiting to be spread out by bulldozers. However, some friends claimed to have climbed up the conveyor belt, when it was not being used, that extended from the unloading shed to the top of the storage shed.

Being so close to the gypsum operation, however, a question took shape in my mind during my early teens: why? The whole operation was a classical example of economic dependency of Canadians being content to be "hewers of wood and drawers of water." Gypsum ore was being cheaply obtained for American processing plants that received much higher returns for the finished product. Why was there no processing plant in Hantsport (or elsewhere nearby)? My question was only further re-enforced in the summer of 1967 when I worked on two of the gypsum ships and saw first-hand four of the American-based processing plants.

This "what-if" question cannot now be answered. Hantsport's gypsum company and operations came to an end a few years ago with massive restructuring changes to the whole world-wide gypsum industry and building construction market. The gypsum sheds are now abandoned most likely providing shelter to raccoons and other vermin; and grass weeds grow on the unused rail tracks. Yes, my former home is now a lot quieter, but closure of the gypsum operations constitutes a gap in the town's economy that has yet to be replaced.

b. Lumber, Pulp, Apples, and "Kisses"

The gypsum operations in Hantsport held little attraction and provided little opportunity for play – mainly operations to watch. Other industries, however, were a mixed bag as to their accessibility. Storage areas rather than heavy machinery and production areas were usually more accessible, such as in the cases of Murray's lumber mill, Minas Basin Pulp and Power company, and the Avon apple juice cannery.

Located on Foundry Road where there is now (in 2017) a playing field for soccer, Murray's had a long history going back to the early part of the 20th century. It had apparently made primarily fruit baskets but that activity was mainly before my time. By the 1950s and early 1960s, only a small portion of the facility's operations was devoted to the production of wooden quart- and pint-sized fruit baskets. My friend, Johnnie, worked there occasionally to make these baskets by stapling very thin slices of wood into a box. Except for going into the small basket-making room where Johnnie showed us how he made fruit baskets, we stayed away from the major part of the mill where large saws cut lumber. Just to see these saws was sufficient warning to stay away – a no play zone.

Outside the production mill, it was a different situation where we could and did play on the stacks of lumber in the storage yard. The planks of lumber were piled alternatively in a three-sided formation, if my memory serves me correctly, so that the spacing allowed the lumber to dry properly. In addition, the three-sided formation created a triangular hole in the centre. These stacks of lumber were thus very inviting to kids. Johnnie: "Come along. They are easy to climb. Just stick your toes in the open areas between the planks."

Stewart: "But, why? What's the purpose of climbing these stacks?"

Laurie: "Well, we can hide in the hole in the centre of each stack."

Johnnie: "Or we can pretend that each stack is a tank. Just like the war movie that we saw a couple of weeks ago. The holes will be like the tank turrets and we can be the commanders in war games."

These stacks of lumber were an accessible playground for much of the year. Meanwhile, the two companies based on pulp production had some serious, heavy-duty equipment. Unless you wished to be grinded to shreds, scalded, baked, or flatted – literally – you walked quickly past these machines.

I was first introduced to the pulp mill – Minas Basin Pulp and Power Company Limited – in the late 1940s. The father of a friend worked at the mill and we used to take a fresh lunch to him each day when he worked the day shift. We went pass the monstrous and noisy machines on our way to the lunch room canteen. I doubt that children would have such easy access to such a dangerous workplace today; in fact, we shouldn't have been permitted at that time. Still, it was a valuable lesson to be so close to those machines; we developed a healthy respect to stay away from them.

The heavy machine production areas of the pulp mill were thus self-imposed no-go areas, except to walk by them. The wharf and storage sheds, however, were different stories. When ships docked to be loaded with pulp, kids would gather to watch the operation and, with a few friends, I would mix "Kool-aid" to sell to the workers. One storage shed was used to store pulp waiting the arrival of ships, and it was an okay play area. The other storage shed – the "Funny-Book Shed" – was where paper products like newspapers, magazines and comics were stored waiting to be recycled into pulp. We used to spend hour after hour in this second shed looking for comic books.

A second but related company based on pulp was the Canadian Keyes Fibre Company Limited, and it was an absolute dud from a kid's perspective. The factory made products that were moulded out of pulp – paper plates, egg cartons, as well as trays for meats, produce, and many other items. Practically all of Keyes Fibre's space was devoted to production equipment; while fork lift trucks seemed to be always active in the storage and shipping areas. It was a great location for high school and university students to find summer jobs, but there was no place within where kids could play.

But nothing could out-draw our attention in autumn like the apple storage bins at the Avon apple juice cannery. These bins were a stand-alone structure away from the main processing part of the plant. As such, they were a prime and easily accessible target for kids after school on their way home. The bins were filled to the top with diverse varieties of apples, so we would stop to raid the apple bins until chased away by the manager or by one of his underlings. (See the separate short story about apple-raiding.)

Besides raiding the Avon apple bins, there were a few individual apple trees scattered around Hantsport that also attracted our attention like fruit magnets. Similarly, there were cherry trees and a few pear trees. But we seemed to draw a line with peach trees which we did not raid. There were very few peach trees in town to start with, and we seemed to recognize the difficulty and expense that growers had in growing peaches. At least, that was the case with my group of friends – we had professional and ethical standards as top-notch raiders of fruit. I cannot say the same for other gangs of kids.

This section on Hantsport's industries cannot be closed without a word about Yeaton's candy factory. It apparently made soft chewy toffees with a molasses taste that were commonly called "kisses." I say "apparently" because, if truth be told, I was never once inside that factory. Actually, although Yeaton's had been a successful enterprise many years previously, in all my years in Hantsport during the '50s and early '60s, I never once saw the factory open its door or in production mode. So as kids, we never had access to free samples if there were any to be obtained. Except, that is, on Dominion Day (July 1) celebrations when during the street parade kisses and other candies were tossed to on-lookers. I do not know how this was done, possibly a herd of munchkins or leprechauns were hired to work over night under the moon light to prepare the candy for the following day's parade.

c. Assorted Businesses

While the industries were the backbone of the community, employing hundreds of people, several businesses or small-scaled entities provided necessary support services. We spent time as customers or more commonly just looked at items in these alternative locations.

Most days at lunch time on our way home from school, we would stop at the Post Office to pick up the family's mail. The postal clerks knew each of us and gave us our mail if there was any, even if we had no key for the postal box. As well, we always had a friendly chat with the clerks, especially Gibby Veniot when he was the post master as well as our Boy Scout leader. Mail delivery was especially exciting at Xmas time, because relatives in England always sent parcels that contained unique British chocolates and candies that were not available locally at that time in Nova Scotia.

Directly opposite the Post Office at the corner of William and Station Streets, there was the Sears catalogue shopping office. People would order items from the Sears catalogue, and then pick up their ordered items within a few days time. If a customer was not satisfied with the delivered item, it could easily be returned through the same store. Mrs. Fuller, a wonderful lady who was also our Wolf Cub leader in the early 1950s, was the store's manager for many years. As well, for a time, my mother worked at this store as well. Shopping patterns have since changed, and Sears has curtailed its catalogue shopping and pick-up service in small towns across Canada. People are now more likely to shop now by running around, at their own expense and effort, to different store locations. Or now with the Internet, online shopping is growing in popularity.

Many other small businesses were fixtures of the town by providing invaluable services, and their owners were well-liked community leaders. Mr. L. B. Harvie and his son, John, operated Hantsport's major grocery store; Mr. Carl Dowe's convenience store had the best, and most delicious, display of penny candy in town; and the movie theatre manager was always willing in his spare time to show us how the projection machines worked. Mr. George MacBurnie possessed an endless information storehouse about baseball that he freely shared as he gave haircuts. Mr. Dave Freeman's electrical store was the only place in town where you could purchase records of popular songs for record players The Slack hardware store had an excellent collection of miniature *Dinky* cars that closely resembled real cars. The *"5¢ to $1"* department store was remarkably small even for its time, but always seemed to have what you were looking for. There was also for a brief time the Cozy Corner restaurant, at the corner of William and Oak Streets which was run by the Hazlett family when my family first arrived; it was then acquired and operated by Ron and Irene Johnson until it was destroyed in a fire.

d. Boy Scout Paper Collection

Long before recycling became fashionable at the turn of the 21st century, the Minas Basin Pulp and Power Company's paper mill had the capacity to recycle paper. This had long been the practice when somebody came up with the idea that the town's Boy Scout association could raise funds by collecting used paper on Saturday mornings to be sold to the paper mill. The mill also agreed to provide the Boy Scouts with a truck and driver to help us to pick up the paper; as well, the mill paid us something like $20 per ton of paper. This money was a major source of our financing, and was used to fund our troop's activities including the sending of scouts to a summer camp. At the time, Gibby Veniot was our Boy Scout leader, probably the only adult who we called by their given name. Everybody in town knew Gibby as he was both the post master and a home-town star player with the town's senior-level baseball team, the *Hantsport Shamrocks* (see Brian Bishop's book of 2015).

The paper collection project got off to a slow and rough start sometime in the early 1950s. As we spread out across the town early on a Saturday morning for the first time, it seemed that a lot of residents were unaware of the collection of used paper. We got more than one angry response from residents at being awaken at 9 or 10 on a Saturday morning by some snotty nosed kids in Boy Scout uniforms looking for used paper. But after a few weeks, the Boy Scout paper collection became a fixture in the town. We even had regular customers who conscientiously saved paper all week long in anticipation for our weekly visit.

The most eagerly awaited part of the paper collection, however, came with the truck pick-up starting at 11 AM. We would jump on and off the back of the truck to pick up the small piles of paper that we had collected earlier in the morning. I now shudder to think about all the jumping on and off the truck that we did. It is a wonder that nobody broke his neck or run over. In fact, the jumping would not be permitted today; neither would be the practice of driving around with kids unsecured on top of paper in bins on the back of a truck.

Between pick-up spots, we would rummage through the collected paper looking especially for magazines that our own families did not subscribe to. The *Star Weekly* was the name of the most searched for magazine. It used to have fantastic pictures of National Hockey League hockey players – large and glossy pages that we took home to attach to our bedroom walls.

In addition to the hockey pictures, we sometimes acquired other items. For example, the *5¢ to $1* department store and some other businesses were regular stops on the pick-up route. Once, I found a slightly broken stapler that had carelessly found its way into the paper to be recycled. I quickly fixed the stapler with an elastic band, and after sixty years, it is still in working condition on my desk (six inches away as I type).

Hantsport's diverse industries and several businesses were integral features during the 1950s and early '60s. Hundreds of adults, of course, worked at these locations, while children grew up within their presence. Sometimes children simply observed the operations; other times, we played in the non-production storage areas eating apples, reading funny books, or just fooling around. We got to know these facilities better than some of the managers and workers. Some of us even became full- or part-time workers at these establishments. Above all, we became aware of the diverse opportunities in life and the value of hard work, and to do the job well no matter what it may be. That was the reality of Hantsport during the '50s and early '60s – the Town of Industries.

11

CASINO HANTSPORT

Money was never plentiful while growing up in the 1950s and early 1960s. Children were thus always on the look out to gain an extra penny or two, either by work or through good fortune.

Today's (2017) political economists often refer to the prosperity of the post-war era. I am not certain about that interpretation because the nature of the economy was so different at that time compared to now. It was more of a "meat and potato" economy in which what little money there was went for basics like food, clothing, housing, transportation, and to pay doctor bills, with scant little being spent on discretionary expenditures.

Our parents had grown up during the "dirty '30s" followed by the rationing of the World War II years. My mother especially had experienced the hard times of England during the war years when practically everything was in short supply if not completely unavailable. Parents thus knew how to handle their household expenditures, buying groceries and other store-bought items on credit, re-using jars for their own preserving and pickling, doing home repairs when things broke or needed patching or making Christmas gifts for the children.

So as children, we never went without want for basics. It was an era of meals at the family table, no fast-food restaurants or pizza pick-ups. Clothes that had been out grown by one child would be passed down to the next child. Holes in clothing were darned, and tears would be stitched. But we were healthy and comfortable. In a way, this resourceful, enterprising spirit of our parents rubbed off onto us, the baby boomers. However, there was also a desire for discretionary money that became an aching desire as years advanced and we became more independent.

By the early 1950s, the twenty-five cent allowance that many of us earned for doing weekly household chores never seemed to go very far. Most of that allowance was spent on the Saturday afternoon movie or perhaps a night out at Don's restaurant on Main Street. We must have driven Don's staff crazy when four or six young boys entered on a Friday or Saturday evening. We would occupy a whole booth while hardy spending a cent, not to mention playing tricks like putting salt in the white sugar container and white sugar in the salt shaker. One of us would order French fries or a bottle of pop to justify all of us occupying the booth; once finished, another would order his fill, and so on. Even by the late '50s when our allowances had increased to a dollar or two, the allowance money never seemed to be enough. This was no doubt partly due to the opening of a pool room/restaurant on Davison Street. We used to idle away our time by going to the pool room on weekends, and by going to local dances or held in a neighbouring town.

In any case, we always had to be resourceful to find other money to supplement our allowances. Perhaps five or more boys in town at the time were really lucky because they had paper delivery routes. I don't know how much they made by delivering newspapers, but it always seemed to be like a money tree for the rest of us. No doubt our imaginations far exceeded reality. Nevertheless, it was always necessary for most of us to look elsewhere for money.

We learned early in life the value of empty pop bottles, about one or two cents for a small pop bottle and five cents for a large-sized pop bottle. So we always had our eyes open for discarded pop bottles that we could immediately turn into cash at a grocery store or a convenience store.

Carl Dowe's convenience store, next to Harvie's grocery store on William Street, was a favourite location in our neighbourhood. Not only did Mr. Dowe accept pop bottles but he had a large, glass-enclosed case of penny apiece candy: individual caramels, chocolates, bubblegum, suckers, and, for a bit more, licorice (look-alike) cigarettes, cigars and pipes. Mr. and Mrs. Dowe must have had to wipe kid drool and finger smudges off that case every evening!

Besides pop bottles, there was really big money to be made in retrieving beer bottles. Since there was no liquor store in Hantsport at that time, it was necessary to accumulate a few dozen beer bottles before convincing one of our fathers to drive us to the redeeming centre in Windsor, seven miles away, for several dollars per trip.

It was Victor, however, who introduced me to the fact that in suitable weather there was a weekly old-time country dance at the outdoor dance-stand located on the Community Centre grounds. As Victor explained, "each morning after the dance, it is like a gold mine with beer and pop bottles plus loose change scattered all over the grounds of the Community Centre. Last week, I picked up $7.50 in bottles and found $2.65 in lost change." Since Victor lived on Porter's Avenue next to the Community Centre, he was always able to arrive at that location before I could and thus he had first picking. So there was no way that I could compete at the Community Centre location.

Fortunately, however, the dancers and party goers also went to what was then a vacant piece of land called the Point over-looking the Avon River. Located at the corner of Avon Street and Tannery Road, the Point was a favourite spot for the merry makers to continue their drinking and related carousing activities. A "make-out" point, if there ever was one! This location was much closer to where I lived, so I would jump onto my bicycle at around six in the morning to head for this secluded spot, returning with a dozen or more beer bottles in my bicycle carrier. Within a month or two, I had a few dozen pint and quart beer bottles (as they were then sold) for a trip to the Windsor redeemer.

Bottle collection was not the only source of extra revenue, however. On one occasion, Laurie and I decided to become big-time entrepreneurs – businessmen by another name as we learned. This came at a time when we had just made some money through returning beer bottles. Our bright idea was to buy candy and chocolate bars at Dowe's convenience store; we would then divide the goods into individual pieces to be hauled around town in my cart to be sold to other kids. The plan seemed to work as we had sold all of the candy by the end of the day. However, we had the exact same amount of money as we had started the day. Nobody had ever told us about marking up the original cost in order to make a profit. We had simply sold every item at the same price that we had paid. We were not greedy enough to sell penny candy for two pennies to our close friends!

On another occasion, money (nickels, dimes, and quarters) fell to the ground around us, almost like manna from heaven. No work, no effort on our behalf, just money falling all around us. This was in the early fifties around springtime just after the Cozy Corner restaurant, which was located on William Street at the corner of Oak Street and directly opposite to the movie theatre on the other side of William, was destroyed due to a fire. It so happened that Ray and Irene Johnson owned the establishment, and along with their children (Laurie, Darrell, and Diane) lived above the restaurant. I was staying at the Johnsons at that time, and have the vaguest recollection of being rescued by firefighters. While still half asleep, the firefighters passed me from one to another to a nearby house where I continued to sleep for the remainder of the night.

Eventually, Ray and Irene gave Laurie and me the destroyed large-size jukebox – it was essentially just the shell of the jukebox as the records and electrical mechanisms inside had been melted in the fire. As Laurie said, "we can knock out the ragged glass edges of the window in the top half and take out the melted stuff in the bottom. Then we can climb inside the shell, close the door, kneel down, and put on puppet shows through the above window hole. It will be just like the 'Punch and Judie' puppet shows that they have in England."

I replied, "Okay, let's take the jukebox to the barn behind my house where we can work on it."

Laurie and I began to drag the jukebox down William Street over the railroad tracks and across the street to my house when the unexpected happened. With each twist and turn as we tugged and pushed the burnt-out jukebox, an endless stream of coins began to tingle-jangle to the ground. Obviously, the coins came from the metal container that had not melted in the fire and was located in a secured position. Such an unexpected bonanza happens perhaps at best once in a kid's lifetime, and that was ours.

It was far more typical for us, however, to raise money through bottle collection. Alternatively, we would pick cherries in the spring and blackberries in late summer to sell door-to-door. On yet other occasions, we would order a carton of Christmas cards or vegetable seeds from a comic book advertisement, and then sell them to neighbours. Once we became teenagers, however, we felt that we could earn money by doing more manly things.

When a pulp ship came in, a few of us would go to the wharf early in the morning in hope of being hired to operate a cart hauling bales of pulp from the storage shed to the side of the boat. Despite our personal feelings of bravado, we would not have lasted half-an-hour because each hand cart was heavy by itself not to mention that each bale probably weighed 750-plus lbs. Consequently, we were never hired. Still the opportunity of working at the pulp ship was not completely lost, at least not in the summertime. We would scurry up the road to my home and make "Kool-Aid", which we then sold for five cents per glass to workers at the ship. Lemon lime seemed to have been the favourite flavour although the men kept asking for something stronger, whatever that might have been.

Although earning money was the usual way to supplement our weekly allowance, we eventually became aware of another means: gambling. The '50s and early '60s were a time of change not in terms of just technologies and realities but also in values, and this was especially the case with gambling. Today, since the late 1960s and 1970s, gambling has slowly but surely become a regular and open feature of life. Lottery tickets are sold at shopping mall kiosks and retail stores, poker games are shown daily on television, and various gambling venues are available everywhere through the Internet. But in the fifties, gambling was still illegal under the Criminal Code and, perhaps more importantly, it was considered to be a social taboo.

There were always a few exceptions to the legality rule, however, such as the weekly bingo game at the Roman Catholic Church, and the games of chance at the Community Centre's fair grounds on July 1st when we celebrated Dominion Day (now called Canada Day). These were considered to be exceptions, not only in Hantsport but across Canada, because the money raised was small scale and then it was used for public benefit or for charity. Another exception was in respect to local community social activities. For example, many of our parents would gather once per week alternating from one home to another to play Rummoli or card games for pennies. Of course, in our parents' minds, this was not gambling but just a pleasant social evening together, especially during long, cold winter nights. Similarly, when as kids we started to play Blackjack, it was seen as just entertainment and not gambling, especially since we usually did not play for money. It was just a game like playing marbles to see who could out skill everybody else, even when we played for keeps where the winner kept the marbles.

At least, that was the way it was until the summer of 1954 when about twelve of us went with other Hants county Boy Scouts to a camp located at Point Prim, Prince Edward Island. Ronnie was our natural leader to whom we all looked up to, even though he was only a couple of years older than the rest of us.

Ronnie's savvy skills became immediately apparent when, on arrival at the camp site, he successfully negotiated with the adult camp directors that one of the only two tents that had already been erected would be given to the Hantsport troop. We would not have the hassle of erecting a tent. The second part of the deal was that our troop would not have to do "kitchen patrol," where the boys of each tent rotated daily in washing dishes and preparing meals. By coincidence, because of rain on the day of departure, we were also spared the drudgery of taking down our tent. In return, Ronnie committed our troop to gathering daily the firewood for the kitchen and for the evening's bomb fire, about fifteen minutes of work per day. Talk about a sweet deal; what was put into the directors' hot chocolate to let us off so lightly?

But Ronnie was not one to relax on his negotiation laurels with camp directors. He had bigger fish to fry. Along with another boy working as a secret partner, the two went around the camp to flip pennies. "Hey, Jan, how would you like to flip pennies? Each of us will flip one penny, just the three of us. Whoever tosses a side not flipped by the other two will win all three pennies. Nothing can be easier."

To which after winning the first flip, Jan replied, "you are right, that was easy and I just won two pennies. Let's have another flip." Of course, given the odds, the two partners soon cleaned out Jan, and much of the remainder of the camp soon followed. Flipping coins, however, turned out to be small potatoes on the gambling scene.

It started as normal, friendly card games with Blackjack (also called "21") being the favourite game. Blackjack was a very quick game and easy to understand: each player is dealt two cards with the second card being dealt face up for all to see, and then a player has the opportunity to ask for additional cards. To win, it is necessary to have a combined value of 21, or to be the closest to that number without going over, or to have five cards valued 21 or less.

At the start, these games were friendly games, not for money, just as had been the usual practice at home. Then somebody suggested that each player should wager a penny for each game with the winner taking the pot. Even when some boys played poker, a penny wager often became the norm, although occasionally it went up to a five cent wager. Once money entered the picture, I stopped playing because I only had five dollars in total and it had to cover treats on the way to and from the camp plus expenses for a scheduled visit to a fair in a nearby town.

However, boys from other tents with money burning in their pockets would make their way to our tent, better known as Casino Hantsport. It was an eye-opening sight to watch the calculating strategies, the exchange of money, and the comings-and-goings of players. But our eyes really bugged out over the $5 game.

One regular player was particularly successful, taking pot after pot, much to the annoyance of another regular player. Eventually, this annoyed player lost patience and suggested putting aside the measly "penny" games, and settle matters once and for all as to who was the better gambler by playing for big money. Both players wagered five dollars each, and the usual winner was successful once again. Perhaps more than anything else, this $5 game firmly established our tent's reputation as Casino Hantsport. Just how great this reputation was, however, did not really hit us until a few days later.

I don't know how it happened because we didn't have access to a telephone for somebody to make a long-distance call. Also, this camp in the early '50s was obviously held long before the Internet, cell phones and text messaging. But somehow or other, news about Casino Hantsport got home before we did. Parents were furious to learn that their little "Johnnie" angels had become big time gamblers. And it had taken place under the protective supervision of the Boy Scouts of Canada!

Not only did parents pounce upon us as we got off the bus, but they had already vented their words to Gibby Veniot (our local Scout master) even though he had not been with us at this camp. We never found out who the squealer was, but we certainly felt bad that blame was misplaced upon Gibby. Many of us would not have afforded going to camp if it hadn't been for Gibby's fund-raising initiatives. Of course, the heated public temperature eventually cooled down, and Hantsport Casino soon became a forgotten event.

"Follow the money" is often the investigative technique used by police detectives to solve crimes in the movies and television mysteries. The same words of advice could be followed to track our development as youngsters – just track how we acquired money. When weekly allowance money for doing chores became insufficient, we searched for alternative sources. Earning money was the natural path to follow in a working class town. Whether it was redeeming bottles, picking and selling berries, mowing neighbour's lawns, selling "Kool-Aid," or whatever other work was available. The basics and values of hard work had been firmly instilled in us by our parents as had the enterprising drive to become self-sufficient.

Yet we lived at a most intriguing time during the '50s and early '60s. Traditional values and ways of thinking were being stretched and challenged in many walks of life. Gambling was a case in point. We were willing to break this traditional social taboo, as was evident with Casino Hantsport, as long as it was small scale and based on mutual consent.

ANNOTATED BIBLIOGRAPHY

(Assorted background sources that relate either particularly to Hantsport or in general to the Annapolis Valley, Nova Scotia, and the Maritime Provinces.)

- Bishop, Brian H. 2015. *Barbershop Baseball: A History of the Hantsport Shamrocks.* Hantsport, N. S.: Self-published and printed by Friesens Corporation.

  Brian and I grew up and went to school together. His book provides a thorough historical account of baseball in Hantsport, which was such a big part of the town's life both on and off the playing field over the years including the 1950s and early 60s.

- Bruce, Harry. 1981. *R. A.: The Story of R. A. Jodrey, Entrepreneur.* Toronto: McClelland and Stewart Limited.

  Roy A. Jodrey (perhaps better known as "R. A.") was not only Hantsport's most significant entrepreneur during the middle part of the 20th century, but his reputation extended throughout the region as well as nationally and internationally. This volume is a weighty yet insightful account of the man and his economic endeavours.

- Buckler, Ernest. 1989 [1952]. *The Mountain and the Valley.* Afterword by Robert Gibbs. Toronto: McClelland and Stewart.

Ernest Buckler was a renowned writer of fiction – mainly short stories and a few novels – about the Annapolis Valley region in western Nova Scotia. The Mountain and the Valley was his first and most widely recognized novel, depicting a romanticized view of rural life in the Annapolis Valley mainly during the first half of the 20th century.

- Chittick, Hattie. 1964 [1968]. *Hantsport on Avon.* Revised Edition. Hantsport, N. S.: Hantsport Women's Institute.

Originally prepared for the Hantsport Women's Institute in 1940, a second edition was released in 1954 with a revised edition released in 1964. The Hantsport Memorial Community Centre then released a reprinting of the revised edition as a "tribute" to Hattie Chittick in 1968. Despite these later editions, the bulk of the book's contents do not appear to have changed much since the original 1940 edition. In any case, Chittick delivers a mish-mash of facts – mainly loosely connected memories and selected facts – of the town's original leading families and personalities, ship-building history, and various events.

- Gloade, Harold. 1988. *As I Remember: Hantsport Area in the 30s.* Hantsport, N. S.: Lancelot Press.

Not all of Gloade's memories are about Hantsport; many are about the rural-forested area of Bishopville on the outskirts of Hantsport. The author nevertheless delivers several lucid accounts of Hantsport and the people of the area during the 1930s.

- Gloade, Harold. n. d. *As I Remember: Hantsport Area in the 30s, Book Two.* Hantsport, N. S.: Lancelot Press.

See the above annotation for Gloade's first booklet, as this second booklet is essentially a continuation of the initial publication.

- Hantsport and Area Historical Society. 1995. *Hantsport, 1895-1995 – 100th Anniversary of Incorporation Calendar.* Hantsport, N. S.: Hantsport and Area Historical Society's Centennial Project.

This calendar is being mentioned because it presents several fascinating photographs from the past with descriptive captions that provide a sense of place, or the "look" of the town during its first hundred years of incorporation. [Of related interest as part of Hantsport's centennial celebrations, note paper with sketches mainly of different buildings was printed by Nova Graphics, located in Dartmouth, N. S.]

- Kalkman, Tony. 2000. *Along the Tracks of the Dominion Atlantic and the Halifax and South Western Railways*. Kentville, N. S.: Kentville Publishing.

The Dominion Atlantic was the name of the railroad that operated from Halifax down through the Annapolis Valley, going through Hantsport. This collection of black-and-white postcards and photographs illustrates the importance of trains in western Nova Scotia especially during the early 1900s, albeit by the 1950s, railroads were beginning to face major challenges posed by highway transportation. The two pictures on pp. 51 and 52 relate specifically to Hantsport.

- Paris, Jr., John, with Robert Ashe. 2014. *They Called Me Chocolate Rocket*. Halifax, N. S.: Formac Publishing Company Limited.

John Paris came from the neighbouring town of Windsor, seven miles away from Hantsport, and we met on the playing field many times. As his book relates, after several set-backs, John persevered to become hockey's first black professional coach to lead his team to winning his league's championship (the Atlanta Knights of the Central Hockey League in 1994). For our purpose, however, John's account reveals the spirit of individual initiative combined with an equally strong sense of social responsibility and respect for others that we had as baby boomers in the Valley during the '50s and '60s.

- Parker, Mike. 2006. *Historic Annapolis Valley: Rural Life Remembered*. Halifax, N. S.: Nimbus Publishing Limited.

Through text and photographs, Mike Parker delivers a most exhaustive account of society and economy of the Annapolis Valley, especially its numerous small-towns and rural setting, primarily from the late 19th century until the late 20th century. It is an invaluable storehouse of well-researched information for both those with roots in the Valley as well as for those from away.

- Pollard, David. 2010. *Ships & Sails: Hantsport Tales*. Altona, Manitoba: Self-published and printed by Friesens Corporation.

This book appears to be a self-published publication. Despite its intriguing title, the text comes across as mainly a series of rants and unconnected ramblings that have little to do with Hantsport. Just the same, the astute reader will find some factual insights about the community as well as a plethora of rare photographs from the late 19th and early 20th centuries.

- Sircom, Hilary, ed. 2001. *Talk about the Valley: Stories from Nova Scotia's Annapolis Valley – Norman Creighton*. Halifax, N. S.: Nimbus Publishing Limited.

Norman Creighton (and, to a lesser extent, his brother, Alan) lived for several years in Hantsport from the 1930s until the 1990s, although I never met or knew them. The former wrote numerous documentary-styled stories mainly for CBC radio, which have been transcribed for this collection as edited by Hilary Sircom. Unlike the memories of the Chittick and Gloade booklets, the Norman Creighton documentary stories deliver an invaluable, well-researched account of individuals, towns, and pattern of life primarily during much of the 20th century in the Annapolis Valley. I can easily recognize, however, that many of his Valley stories are either explicitly or implicitly centred on Hantsport.

- Walsh, Christopher A. 2010. *Under the Electric Sky: The Legacy of the Bill Lynch Shows*. Lawrencetown Beach, N. S.: Pottersfield Press.

This book is a fascinating account of the Maritime-owned and -based Bill Lynch carnival shows (consisting of rides, games of chance, food concessions, and other amusements). The Lynch shows used to travel each summer from community to community to set up at exhibitions and fairs throughout the Maritime Provinces from the mid-1920s until the end of the twentieth century. Walsh provides a window on the importance that the annual fair/carnival had in the towns and cities of the region. Hantsport had its annual fair on Dominion Day (now called Canada Day), and it is difficult to grasp the rhythm of life of Hantsport without acknowledging the start of summer signaled by the annual fair and related events (such as the street parade, opening of the community swimming pool, and Dick Beazley races) each and every July 1.

www.ingramcontent.com/pod-product-compliance
Lightning Source LLC
Chambersburg PA
CBHW021120130626
46554CB00002B/784